For my mum, my No.1 fan.

Ching-He Huang is an Emmy-nominated TV chef and cookery author. Born in Taipei, Taiwan, her culinary ethos is to use fresh, organic, ethically sourced ingredients to create modern dishes that fuse Chinese tradition with innovation and are accessible for home cooks. Her immensely popular TV series include *Chinese Food Made Easy*, *Chinese Food in Minutes*, *Exploring China* and *Ching's Amazing Asia*. She has also been a regular guest chef on *Saturday Kitchen* and *Lorraine*.

Ching has written seven bestselling cookbooks: *Eat Clean: Wok Yourself to Health*, *Exploring China*, *Ching's Fast Food*, *Everyday Easy Chinese*, *Ching's Chinese Food in Minutes*, *Chinese Food Made Easy* and *China Modern*. She is also the creator of The Lotus Wok – a wok with a dynamic nano-silica coating for high performance cooking. Ching divides her time between the UK, the US and Asia.

STIR CRAZY

100 Deliciously Healthy
Stir-fry Recipes

Ching-He Huang

Photography by Tamin Jones

Kyle Books

First published in Great Britain in 2017 by
Kyle Books, an imprint of Kyle Cathie Ltd
192-198 Vauxhall Bridge Road
London SW1V 1DX
general.enquiries@kylebooks.com
www.kylebooks.co.uk

10 9 8 7 6 5 4 3 2 1

ISBN 978 0 85783 426 3

Editor: Judith Hannam
Editorial Assistant: Hannah Coughlin
Copy Editor: Barbara Dixon
Nutritionist: Cordelia Woodward
Designer: Caroline Clark
Photographer: Tamin Jones
Food Stylist: Aya Nishimura
Prop Stylist: Wei Tang
Production: Nic Jones and Gemma John

A Cataloguing in Publication record for this title is
available from the British Library.

Colour reproduction by ALTA London
Printed and bound in China by C&C Offset Printing Co., Ltd.

Hello!

Thanks so much for choosing *Stir Crazy*. I hope it will inspire you to pick up the wok and have some fun when it comes to those all-important mealtimes!

Stir Crazy is a collection of delicious stir-fry recipes that I designed with busy people like you in mind. They are for all occasions and simple enough for everyday healthy cooking at home, with nutrition, taste, affordability and balance in mind.

I've written a handful of books on Chinese cookery and being a Chinese cookery expert I always get asked the same questions: 'How do I make a really good stir-fry so the veggies are crisp and fresh and don't go all soggy?' 'I make stir-fries at home all the time but it's so boring, what flavours can I try?' 'What sauces can I make?' 'What tips and tricks can you offer?'

If these are the questions plaguing your everyday kitchen/stir-fry needs, then this is the book for you. I demystify the art of making a good stir-fry and offer you tips on getting it right. Whether it's a saucy dish or a crispy dry-fry, whether you are a vegetable or meat lover, a novice or an experienced cook, here is a varied and wide range of dishes that I hope will help you increase your stir-fry repertoire.

So let's get started...and happy wokking!

Love,

Ching xx

Mastering the wok

Why stir-fry?

Stir-frying is quick and it's easy to start, but it is not always so easy to master. Learning what separates a good stir-fry from a great one takes time and the willingness to do a 'wok dance' (see page 9)! It is all about the timing – knowing when to add what and how to get the best out of each ingredient.

Stir-frying can also be inexpensive and by cooking on a concentrated heat with a small amount of oil you retain more of the nutrients, yet the heat helps to break down the fibres, making it easier for you to digest the food and absorb the nutrients.

This way of cooking is fun, fast and can be healthy too, depending on what type of dish you are making and what you are putting into it.

Why use a wok?

This 2,000-year-old magical cooking pot is a way of life all over Asia and is used for sautéing, braising, frying and steaming. It can be a challenge cooking for family mealtimes and an express tool such as this clever vessel can be a lifesaver on busy days. It is the ultimate stir-fry implement!

How do I go about choosing a wok?

If you are really into healthy eating, I would suggest a stainless steel wok. It can be seasoned with coatings of apple cider vinegar, each coating evaporated to give a clear, thin non-stick layer. However, stainless steel as a material sometimes has uneven heat spots and food can stick, plus it doesn't retain heat as well as carbon steel.

Most professional Chinese chefs use unseasoned carbon steel woks but they need a lot of love and care or they rust. Non-stick varieties, however, are not ideal since the coating comes off with time. Some carbon steel woks have a flat, wide base more like a saucepan, which is not a traditional wok shape, so look for ones with deep sides (to allow you to toss the food) and a small centre (to concentrate the heat). Traditional woks are round-bottomed but these require a wok ring set over your stove, which is another added piece of equipment and not ideal for the modern home, especially induction hobs, which many homes have now.

Aluminium woks are inexpensive but they can rust and warp and are not as good conductors or retainers of heat as carbon steel woks.

My grandmother used to cook on a cast-iron wok and they are the best, but they are extremely heavy and it can be difficult to toss the food or manoeuvre them away from the hob when the heat gets too hot.

Whatever wok you have, however, I always say it's best to use it and not waste it. When it's on its last legs and you need a replacement, please do seek out my Lotus wok. I designed it for people who want a better wok experience. It is inexpensive and is made from carbon steel so that it heats quickly, plus it has a natural, 'non-stick' type, nano-silica coating (made from sand-blasted crystals). It is a medium gauge, so not too heavy yet not flimsy. It's also scratch resistant, so you can use metal utensils on it, and hydrophobic, which means it repels water, giving your veggies that crisp finish, and oleophilic, which means it allows just enough oil to coat the surface of the wok. It is a clever wok that just gets better with time – I have used mine for over two years now and it is still going strong. It comes with a wooden spatula, a glass lid and a stainless steel steamer rack. You can purchase it at www.chinghehuang.com/Lotuswok

Now you have a wok, what's the first step?
If you don't need to season your new wok, you can go right ahead and start cooking – just use a damp sponge and a little soapy water to wash off any industrial oil, dust or dirt, then place on the heat to dry. If you need to season your wok, go to my online video at www.youtube.com/user/chinghehuang, which shows you how.

The 'Breath of the Wok'
I have cooked with a lot of wok masters all over the world and the one thing that differentiates a good stir-fry from a bad one is the 'breath of the wok', a term used to describe the *wok-hei* – the 'smoky flavour' that comes from a good flame-wokked dish and the all-important balance of *xiang*, se, *wei* (the aroma, colour and taste of the overall dish). This is where home wok cooking differs from restaurant wok cooking. Restaurant wok burners can reach heats of 650°C, far higher than the 180°C that the average domestic hob can achieve, although some powerful domestic burners can go as high as 400°C.

Wok chefs in restaurants manoeuvre and operate a gas lever by the side of their legs at the same time as they toss the wok and flick it towards the flames so they lick the sides of the wok, injecting wok smoke into the dish. This is why I have so much respect for wok chefs – they have no fear of the flames, which can sometimes be over 2 metres high. They inject the breath of the wok into the dish, as well as sauté, sear, deep-fry, shallow-fry, steam, braise, all in one cooking vessel, and have the eye-to-hand-to-leg body co-ordination (wok dance) to time the addition of each ingredient perfectly. Cooking on such high heat means that if you are one second out your vegetables lose their shine or crispness and is why perfect stir-frying is so hard to master. Consistent results take practice, timing, skill and unwavering focus. However, this doesn't mean that you can't still get those smoky delicious results from wokking at home! I have some tips to help you.

Stir-fry hacks

Freshness is key

Firstly, arm yourself with the freshest ingredients. If ingredients are substandard you will be able to tell, because vegetables will not look fresh and bright and, once stir-fried, they will go limp very quickly.

Preparation is king – no time to stop and chop

When it's 'wok on', there is no time to do anything – least of all, to stop and chop! So ensure all the ingredients are prepped beforehand and are as close to the wok as possible to save you time.

Size and shape matter

Whenever you add several ingredients to the wok at the same time – for example, aromatics such as garlic, ginger, chillies and small pieces of onion, or different types of vegetable, such as shredded cabbage, carrot and onions – it's important they are all a similar size as this will ensure they cook in the same amount of time.

It's important, too, to consider the size of the main protein ingredient in relation to the rest of the ingredients. For example, if you are wokking beef slices, then make sure the vegetables are cut in slices too, so that the dish looks balanced.

All about the cut

How you cut the ingredients is very important. If you slice on a deep diagonal, it exposes more surface area for cooking and it can also make ingredients go that much further. For example, wafer-thin, square-ish slices can be achieved by slicing across the grain of a cut of beef. Vegetables can be prepared in the same way, so a carrot can be sliced into round coins or into long oval pieces if sliced on the diagonal. Play with the shapes!

'Compartment' cooking

Compartmentalise your ingredients – group aromatics together, also the vegetables, and seasonings. Think of your protein and treat it separately – what flavours are you trying to achieve? Finally, think of your garnishes and ways to inject some freshness into the dish at the end.

What level of heat should I go for?

It's important to get your wok really hot before adding anything, so that you see a little smoke rising off the surface. At that point it's time to quickly add the oil, which will heat up instantly. Heating the wok first means the heat is evenly distributed over the entire surface.

Once you add ingredients to it, the temperature in the wok starts to fall a little, but keep the ingredients moving to prevent them burning or take the wok away from the heat source. If you are really worried about the flame, then heat the wok over a medium-high heat and work your way up to maximum heat over the course of several stir-fries where practice becomes perfect.

The right oils

An odourless, flavourless oil that has a high heat point, such as rapeseed oil, peanut oil or coconut oil, is best – it gives a neutral base on which to create your layers of flavour, yet is able to withstand high temperatures. Toasted sesame oil is really only used for seasoning, unless you deliberately wish to 'burn' the ingredient, such as the ginger in the Taiwanese recipe 'Three cup Chicken' (see page 143).

Balance the aromatics

I like to use a combination of garlic, ginger and chillies – what I call The Holy Trinity – and sometimes I mix and match them with spring onions, shallots and onions. You can also pair some of these, such as garlic and ginger or ginger and chilli. I have been accused of putting garlic, ginger and chillies in almost all my dishes, but this is because I try to inject their healthful, anti-bacterial properties into my cooking as much as possible so that I am getting the maximum nutrients in any one meal. But it is entirely up to you and you can vary what you add to suit your likes and mood.

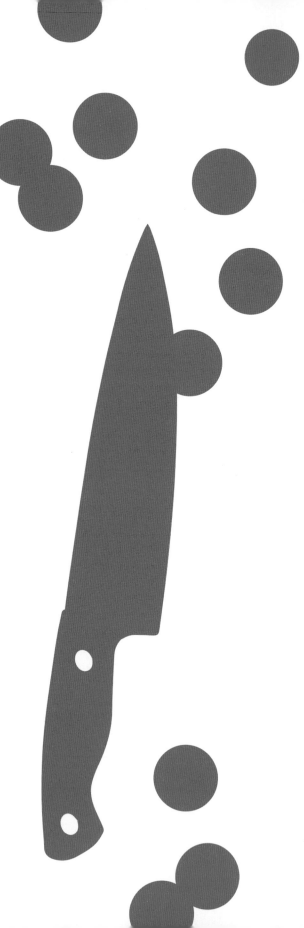

Salt the oil

In my recipes, I sometimes season the oil with a pinch of salt before I add the aromatics. Some chefs swear that this helps to retain the colour of the vegetables. I particularly like this method as it means the salt flavour is evenly distributed throughout, and you are not left with any large, undissolved flakes of salt in the finished dish.

Meats

If you are on a budget, you can make meat go further by using the less expensive cuts. The trick is to use a little bit of baking soda – a couple of very small pinches on a tougher piece of rump steak or pork thighs, for example, will help to tenderise the meat.

My philosophy on meat is to use free-range or organic where possible; yes, it is expensive but I prefer quality over quantity. Personally, I mostly eat vegetable-based stir-fries during the week and so when I do eat meat, I get the good stuff. Eating in this way is a lot healthier (less saturated fat from animal sources), cheaper and better for the environment too. It is up to you whether you go for the cheaper or expensive meat option, just always make sure you season the meat first with a pinch of salt, ground white pepper and a dusting of cornflour to help the meat taste that much juicier. You can also add a pinch of spice, whether Chinese five-spice, turmeric, dried chillies, fennel seeds or ground coriander... just to inject flavour into the meat. You can always taste the difference in the finished dish.

Water is your best friend

When the wok gets too hot to handle, water is your best friend. Having a small jug or glass of water to hand and knowing when to add a drop is important, especially if the wok gets too hot and you are starting to burn the ingredients. If you are making a one-wok dish where you 'don't return' (in Mandarin, *hui guo*) any ingredient to the wok, then you will need to deglaze the wok after cooking individual ingredients and you will need some liquid in between these additions to help each group of ingredients cook. Generally this is after the protein and again once the vegetables have gone in. When stir-frying tender leaf vegetables, after the oil and aromatics have gone in, a small amount of water around the edge of the wok will help to steam-cook the vegetables, ready for seasoning.

Quick homemade sauces and seasonings

From sriracha and oyster to garlic hoisin, you can create sweet, sour, spicy sauces and dressings that will complement your dishes, whether you use them as cook-in sauces or dressings on the side. I have put together several sauce options (see page 19) so that you can mix and match and also pair them with other dishes to suit your taste buds. Feel free to experiment and chop and change – bring out your inner Tom Cruise in *Cocktail* and think of your condiment cupboard like a bar, where you are the mixologist, creating your own sauces and producing a cocktail of stir-fry flavours. Hippy hippy stir shake, fry!

Soybean pastes

I can't live without my soybean pastes, from fermented salted yellow bean (or whole beans in a jar), chilli bean, fermented salted dried black bean (soybeans dried and salted in the sun – just give them a rinse in water, then crush and mix into Shaohsing rice wine to make a paste), to Japanese salty miso paste (which comes in red and white varieties – great for soups, stir-fries, sauces, dressings and marinades), and the Korean chilli paste *gochujang*, which, together with the Korean yellow bean paste, *doenjang*, is one of my favourites. The flavour combinations are limitless, with endless umami (deep savoury) possibilities...

Curry and spice pastes

I love to experiment with South East Asian curry pastes such as Thai red curry, Thai green curry, yellow curry, and so on, and not just to make curry, but for stir-frying and in noodle soups. I also love chilli pastes and sambals from Malaysia, as well as spice mixes and tamarind paste, which give a sour kick and an exotic South East Asian taste to my dishes.

Make it shine

Cornflour or potato flour is an all-important store cupboard ingredient because it helps to bind the flavours in the wok to the protein and vegetables. Traditionally, when cooking meat, a technique called 'velveting' was the norm. It involved coating chicken or beef strips with egg white and cornflour to give the meat a silky texture so retained its juiciness when shallow-fried. However, I've designed a new way to enhance the flavour of the meat without the shallow-frying step – I season the meat first with salt and ground white pepper, then dust with cornflour or potato flour. This helps to seal in the juices as the meat hits the oil in the wok. The trick to making sure it doesn't stick to the wok is to let it brown for 10 seconds and then, once it has some colour, you can easily flip the meat to cook on the other side. Don't worry if the meat catches – those slightly burnt edges all add to the flavour. You can also loosen the flavours in the wok by using a small drop of water or Shaohsing rice wine to deglaze the pan after cooking the meat.

In some of the dishes, the cornflour is also mixed with cold water to create a blended cornflour paste that is usually added at the end of the cooking to thicken the sauce and give it a shine as it comes to the boil.

In many dishes, where I 'compartmentalise' and group ingredients together for a more complex flavour, I like to add the cornflour to the ingredients for the sauce – just ensure that the main liquid in the sauce, whether it's water or vegetable stock, is cold, so that the sauce has not thickened before it's been added to the wok (you want the sauce to thicken and caramelise in the wok, not before in the jug).

Love your dofu or is it tofu?

The Mandarin transliteration is 'dofu', the Japanese is 'tofu'. However, whether you call it dofu or tofu, there is no doubt that it is a good source of protein and contains all nine essential amino acids. It is also an excellent source of iron, calcium, manganese, selenium and phosphorus, and of copper, magnesium, vitamin B1 and zinc. Whether you choose fresh, fried, smoked, firm or soft, tofu offers a great meat substitute for vegan and vegetarian meals and is an important food source for Buddhists – it features heavily in Buddhist Chinese cuisine. Try to get organic tofu or that made from sprouted soy.

Spices

To get the best out your spices, particularly whole spices such as Sichuan peppercorns, first dry toast them in a wok or small pan and then grind them in a pestle and mortar or coffee grinder.

Adding an aromatic flourish

Whether you do so with spring onions, fresh coriander, mint, raw beansprouts, nuts or seeds, Japanese nori seaweed, chilli flakes or a wedge of lemon or lime, adding a fragrant aromatic garnish to your stir-fry at the end will enhance your dish.

> **TIP:** The nutritional analysis of kcal, carbs, protein and fat is per portion.

Rice and nutritious grains

Most dishes, unless a chow mein, pair well with rice. You can also use other grains and pulses mixed into the rice, which is something I do when trying to eat more healthily. For example, I often mix jasmine rice, wild rice and green lentils. At other times I serve plain jasmine rice for comfort, and basmati is a good option for fried rice, as it is more robust. Brown rice is also delicious and high in fibre and can be mixed with jasmine rice, wild rice, and chickpeas to create a different bite.

Noodles

It's best to pre-cook noodles according to the packet instructions, then drain and drizzle some toasted sesame oil over to prevent them from sticking together. For low-carb and wheat-free options, try mung bean noodles, sweet potato noodles, shirataki and rice noodles. I also love the traditional wheat flour noodles, which come in several varieties, such as buckwheat, somen, ramen, udon and egg. Recently, I've discovered high protein organic gluten-free soybean noodles, which are delicious in noodle soups, salads and, of course, stir-fries. Do look out for them.

TIPS: Whenever possible use organic or free-range chicken and eggs as they will taste better. All eggs used in these recipes are medium.

Many dishes are gluten-free if you use tamari instead of light soy sauce.

Order of ingredients

When stir-frying, you want the aromatics to impart their essence into the dish without burning them, the meat to be tender and cooked through, and the vegetables to remain crisp and fresh. The order, therefore, in which each ingredient is added and the timing of each addition is vital. There are so many different stir-fries that it is impossible to give a set blueprint – it really does depend on what you are creating. However, there are a few simple rules and methods which are useful to bear in mind as you wok away and start to improvise.

Vegetable stir-fry
(*Cao Cai*)

1

Heat the wok, add the oil, then the aromatics and stir-fry for a few seconds to impart their aroma.

2

Add the vegetables – the crunchier ones first – and stir-fry for less than a minute. Then add the more tender vegetables, cooking them for less than 30 seconds or until wilted. Add a little water around the edges of the wok to create some steam and aid the cooking process.

3

Then it's quickly onto a seasoning liquid of your choice. Cook for 5 seconds, then give a final toss to ensure a balanced seasoned dish.

Dry meat stir-fry
(*Gan Rou Cao*)

1

Heat the wok, add the oil, then the aromatics, and stir-fry for a few seconds.

2

Add meat slices (seasoned with spices and dredged in cornflour or marinated and dredged in potato flour). Allow the meat to 'settle' (sear on one side) in the wok, before flipping it over to cook on the other side for a few seconds.

3

Deglaze the wok with some Shaohsing rice wine or dry sherry, stock or water, then toss in seasoning ingredients, such as soy sauce, chilli sauce or sesame oil, and cook for 30 seconds. A final toss ensures a balanced seasoned dish. Garnish with fresh herbs (coriander, spring onion or chives) and serve immediately.

Saucy Meat & Veg Stir-fry
(*Gou Chien Rou Cai*)

1

Heat the wok, add the oil, then the aromatics, and stir-fry for a few seconds.

2

Add the meat slices (seasoned with salt, ground white pepper and dredged in potato flour). Allow the meat to 'settle' (sear on one side) in the wok, before flipping it over to cook on the other side for a few seconds.

3

Deglaze the wok with some Shaohsing rice wine or dry sherry, stock or water, then toss in your vegetables (all cut into similar shapes and sizes).

4

Pour in a cup of vegetable stock, add seasoning ingredients, such as light soy sauce, black rice vinegar, toasted sesame oil and chilli sauces. Bring the liquid to the boil, season with cornflour and water paste, and give a final toss to ensure a balanced dish. Garnish with fresh herbs (if using) and serve immediately.

Stir-fry noodles
(*Cao mein*)

1

Heat the wok, add the oil, then the aromatics, and stir-fry for a few seconds.

2

Add the meat slices (seasoned with salt, ground white pepper and dredged in potato flour). Allow the meat to 'settle' (sear on one side) in the wok, before flipping it over to cook on the other side for a few seconds.

3

Deglaze the wok with some Shaohsing rice wine or dry sherry, stock or water, then toss in your vegetables (all cut into similar shapes and sizes).

4

Add the cooked noodles, followed by seasoning ingredients, such as light soy sauce, black rice vinegar, toasted sesame oil or chilli sauce. Stir-fry for 1 minute, mixing all the ingredients well, then give a final toss to ensure a balanced seasoned dish. Garnish with fresh herbs (if using) and serve immediately.

Stir-fry 'Soup' Noodles
(*Tang Mein*)

1

Heat the wok, add the oil, then the aromatics, and stir-fry for a few seconds.

2

Add the meat slices (seasoned with salt, ground white pepper and dredged in potato flour). Allow the meat to 'settle' (sear on one side) in the wok, before flipping it over to cook on the other side for a few seconds.

3

Deglaze the wok with some Shaohsing rice wine or dry sherry, stock or water, then toss in your vegetables (all cut into similar shapes and sizes).

4

Pour in 800ml vegetable stock, add cooked noodles, seasoning ingredients, such as light soy sauce, black rice vinegar, toasted sesame oil or chilli sauce. Bring to the boil, season with cornflour and water paste. Give a final toss and garnish with fresh herbs (if using) and serve immediately.

Fried Rice
(Cao Fan)

1

Heat the wok, add the oil, and scramble some lightly seasoned eggs. Remove from the wok and set aside.

2

Reheat the wok, add more oil, then the aromatics, and stir-fry for a few seconds.

3

Add small pieces of meat (seasoned with salt, ground white pepper or dredged in potato flour). Allow the meat to 'settle' (sear on one side) in the wok, before flipping it over to cook on the other side for a few seconds.

4

Deglaze the wok with some Shaohsing rice wine or dry sherry, stock or water, then toss in finely diced vegetables, and cooked rice, followed by seasoning ingredients, such as light soy sauce, black rice vinegar, toasted sesame oil or chilli sauce. Cook for 1 minute before adding the scrambled egg, then give a final toss to ensure a balanced seasoned dish. Garnish with fresh herbs (if using) and serve immediately.

Saucy tricks

Sesame Oil, Vinegar, Soy Sauce

a.k.a dumpling sauce.

1 part toasted sesame oil
1 part clear rice vinegar
    or cider vinegar
1 part soy sauce

Mix together in a small glass jar or bowl.

Soy Lemon Chilli Oil

Delicious as a dressing.

1 part soy sauce
1 part chilli oil
1 part lemon juice

Mix together in a small glass jar or bowl.

Oyster Sauce Ketchup

Great on a burger or in fried rice.

1 part oyster sauce
1 part ketchup

Mix together in a small glass jar or bowl.

Salty Spicy Sriracha

Use as seasoning in a stir-fry or as a sauce to pour over steamed vegetables.

1 part soy sauce
1 part sriracha chilli sauce

Mix together in a small glass jar or bowl.

Black Rice Vinegar, Chilli and Soy

Use as seasoning for fried rice or chow mein.

1 part Chinkiang black rice
    vinegar or balsamic vinegar
1 part chilli sauce
1 part soy sauce

Mix together in a small glass jar or bowl.

Sesame Soy

Use as seasoning for stir-fried vegetables.

1 part toasted sesame oil
1 part soy sauce

Mix together in a small glass jar or bowl.

Soy Sesame Ginger Miso

Use as a dressing on steamed fish or vegetables.

1 part soy sauce
1 part toasted sesame oil
¼ part freshly grated ginger
1 part miso

Mix together in a small glass jar or bowl.

My top wok tips

Stir-fry to health

The healthiest way to sear food is at a high heat, stir-frying retains the nutrients in food for maximum flavour with minimum effort required.

Steamed not stirred

Steam chicken, fish or tofu together with your favourite vegetables, marinated in a healthy Chinese sauce, for a healthy one-wok supper. If it's easy to cook, you'll be likely to do it again. Consistently eat this way and you'll be beaming with health.

Rice and grains baby

Try to mix several different kinds of rice for texture, flavour and nutrients. I often combine jasmine, brown rice, wild rice and red rice, and sometimes include lentils and chickpeas for maximum protein.

Know your oils

Use a small amount of a good heat-stable oil such as coconut, rapeseed or peanut oil, all of which are perfect for stir-frying on a high heat. Save your virgin olive oils for delicious dressings.

Magic mushrooms

The Chinese are obsessed with dried shiitake mushrooms; not only do they have an earthy, savoury umami flavour, they are also full of minerals and nutrients. So throw them into broths and soups for healthy tonics.

Berry excited

The Chinese goji berry contains essential amino acids, as well as the highest concentration of protein of any fruit. Loaded with vitamin C and carotenoids, it has 21 trace minerals and is also high in fibre. Throw some into a stir-fry or over steamed fish for a sweet pop.

Go nuts

I love to add cashews, pine nuts, walnuts and Brazils to my stir-fries. Nuts contain healthy fats, are high in protein and a good source of minerals and vitamin E, which promotes healthy skin. A small handful in any dish is enough. You can toast or roast your own to give an extra layer of flavour; just step away from the ready-salted variety.

Get fruity and saucy

I like to mix naturally brewed soy with different kinds of fruit juices and fresh or dried chillies for a sweet-savoury spicy taste to my dishes. A great combination is soy sauce, pineapple juice, chilli flakes and honey. You can also use fresh orange juice, grape juice, mango juice and apple juice.

Spice it up

Chinese five-spice, which is made up of cloves, cinnamon, star anise, Sichuan peppercorns and fennel, adds a distinctive pungent, sweet, spicy, bitter and sour note to dishes. Use it to marinate meats – add with soy and olive oil and some cornflour to coat. The spices come with zero calories and are sealed when they hit the wok, giving hot bursts of flavour.

Wok on!

Invest in a good wok. My nano-silica coated Lotus wok (see page 9) does not give off PFOA and PTFE (perfluorooctanoic acid and polytetrafluoroethylene fumes), toxic chemical fumes that are hazardous to the human body, and you only need a small amount of oil to cook up a great tasting meal. It's also hydrophobic, which means it repels water, and oleophilic, which means it absorbs the right amount of oil to keep your veggies crisp and delicious.

Flavoursome toppings

In Mandarin, cooked ingredients that add a bold hit of flavour to dishes are called *zu xiang*. In Taiwanese they are known as *ken pung*. Usually cooked in oil to explode their flavours, they are either incorporated into finished dishes or served as a condiment on the side.

Soy Shiitake Mushrooms

Use dried shiitake mushrooms as they carry the most flavour.

1 tablespoon rapeseed oil
knob of fresh root ginger, peeled and grated
5 small shallots, finely chopped
100g dried shiitake mushrooms, soaked in warm water for 20 minutes, then drained, tough stalks discarded and finely diced
2 tablespoons low-sodium light soy sauce
1 teaspoon toasted sesame oil
pinch of caster sugar

Heat a wok over a high heat until smoking hot and add the rapeseed oil. Add the ginger and shallots and stir-fry for a few seconds, then add the diced shiitake mushrooms and toss for 1 minute until the shallots have softened. Add the light soy sauce and cook on a medium heat until the shallots and mushrooms have absorbed the flavour of the soy and caramelised at the edges. Season with the toasted sesame oil and a pinch of caster sugar. Place in a small bowl and serve with rice and vegetables, or serve some on top of your flavourite chow mein.

Fried Chilli Dried Shrimp

3 tablespoons rapeseed oil
1 red chilli, deseeded and finely chopped
1 spring onion, finely sliced into 1cm rounds
100g dried baby shrimp, soaked in hot water for 20 minutes, then drained, dried and very finely diced
pinch of sea salt flakes
pinch of dried chilli flakes

Heat a wok over a high heat until smoking and add the rapeseed oil. Add the chilli and spring onion and toss for a few seconds to release their aroma. Add the dried baby shrimp and stir-fry for 2 minutes until the shrimp are a little golden at the edges and toasted. Season with the salt and chilli flakes. Spoon out and serve on top of rice, stir-fried vegetables or noodles.

Fried Garlic and Shallots

50g potato flour
pinch of sea salt flakes
pinch of ground white pepper
pinch of vegetable bouillon powder
5 garlic cloves, sliced
5 small shallots, sliced
100ml rapeseed oil

Put the potato flour, some sea salt, white pepper and the bouillon powder into a bowl and mix well. Toss the garlic cloves and shallots in the seasoned flour and sieve out into another bowl.

Add the oil to the wok and heat to 180°C or until a piece of bread dropped in turns golden brown in 15 seconds. Using a small spider or slotted spoon, gently lower the garlic and shallots into the oil. Fry for 20 seconds until golden, then lift out with the spoon and drain on kitchen paper. Season further to taste with salt, pepper and vegetable bouillon powder. Sprinkle on top of meat, shellfish, noodles or fried rice dishes.

Chinese Salted Black Bean Cooked 'Salsa'

This Chinese salsa is not cooked all the way through so you can appreciate the salty bite and flavours of each of the ingredients.

3 tablespoons rapeseed oil
pinch of sea salt flakes
2 garlic cloves, finely chopped
knob of fresh root ginger, peeled and grated
1 red chilli, deseeded and finely chopped
2 spring onions, finely chopped
1 tablespoon fermented salted black beans, rinsed and crushed
2 tablespoons Shaohsing rice wine or dry sherry
1 teaspoon low-sodium light soy sauce

Heat a wok over a high heat until smoking and add the rapeseed oil. Add the salt and let it dissolve. Add the garlic, ginger, chilli and spring onions and toss for a few seconds, then add the fermented salted black beans and toss for 1 minute to release their aroma. Add the Shaohsing rice wine or dry sherry and season with the light soy sauce. Delicious over fish, chicken and wok-fried beef, or added to noodles, vegetables and rice dishes.

Braised Red-cooked Sweet and Sour Shallots

10 baby mini shallots, left whole
400ml cold water
100ml cold vegetable stock
50ml low-sodium light soy sauce
1 tablespoon Chinkiang black rice vinegar or balsamic vinegar
1 teaspoon dark soy sauce
2 tablespoons brown sugar
1 cinnamon stick
1 star anise

Heat the wok over a medium heat, then add all the ingredients at once and cook for 20 minutes until the liquid has reduced by half and the shallots are soft and tender but still hold their shape. Remove the cinnamon stick and star anise. Serve with rice, vegetables or noodles.

Pickles & chilli sauces

You can add these on the side to pimp up your stir-fries. And why not try some pickles and chilli sauces – easy to make and full of flavour.

Sichuan Garlic Cucumber 'Pickle'

4 small cucumbers, halved lengthways and cut into half-moon slices
1 tablespoon toasted white sesame seeds

For the marinade
2 garlic cloves, grated
50ml clear rice vinegar or cider vinegar
50ml mirin
pinch of ground dry-toasted Sichuan peppercorns
pinch of dried chilli flakes
1 teaspoon chilli oil
pinch of sea salt flakes

Mix all the ingredients for the marinade in a small jug. Place the cucumbers on a shallow tray/bowl, pour the marinade over them and pickle for 10 minutes. Serve on top of fried noodles, rice, meat or shellfish.

Fried Chilli Okra

2 tablespoons rapeseed oil
3 green chillies, deseeded and finely chopped
100g okra, sliced into 5mm coins
1 tablespoon Shaohsing rice wine or dry sherry
2 tablespoons low-sodium light soy sauce
1 tablespoon Chinkiang black rice vinegar or balsamic vinegar
pinch of caster sugar

Heat a wok over a high heat until smoking and add the rapeseed oil. Add the chillies and toss for a few seconds to release their aroma. Add the okra and cook for less than 1 minute. Season with the rice wine, soy sauce, vinegar and caster sugar and cook for 30 seconds until the okra is tender, yet still has a slight bite and the liquid in the wok has reduced. Serve on rice or noodles, or toss some into your favourite steamed greens.

Sweet and Sour Tomato 'Sambal'

2 garlic cloves, crushed
knob of fresh root ginger, peeled and roughly chopped
2 red chillies, seeds in, roughly chopped
1 tablespoon tomato purée
1 tablespoon low-sodium light soy sauce
2 tablespoons agave syrup
1/2 teaspoon dried chilli flakes
50ml cold water
2 tablespoons rapeseed oil
pinch of sea salt flakes
lime juice

Put the garlic, ginger, chillies, tomato purée, soy sauce, agave syrup, chilli flakes and water into a food processor and pulse to a paste.

Heat a wok over a medium heat and add the oil, then the paste and simmer for 2–3 minutes. Season to taste with salt and lime juice.

Serve on the side of your favourite stir-fry.

Sweet and Sour
Plum Daikon

2 ripe plums, stoned and finely
    chopped
1 tablespoon caster sugar
1 star anise
juice of ¹/₂ lime
200g daikon, peeled and grated

Pour 200ml water into a
pan and add the plums, sugar
and star anise. Bring to the
boil, then turn down the heat
to a simmer and cook for
10 minutes. Remove from the
heat. Place the ingredients in
a sieve over a bowl and collect
the plum sauce, then stir in
the lime juice.

Put the daikon in a shallow
bowl, pour the sweet and sour
plum sauce over it and leave
for 10 minutes to pickle. Serve
with fried spicy dishes for a
fresh sweet and sour bite.

Vegetables

Wok-fried Cauliflower with Honey Soy Hoisin and Pine Nuts

1 tablespoon rapeseed oil
1 head of cauliflower, washed and
    broken into florets

For the sauce
1 teaspoon freshly grated peeled
    root ginger
1 red chilli, deseeded and
    finely chopped
1 teaspoon runny honey
1 tablespoon hoisin sauce
1 teaspoon low-sodium light
    soy sauce
50ml cold vegetable stock
1 tablespoon cornflour combined
    with 2 tablespoons cold water

For the garnish
handful of toasted pine nuts
handful of finely chopped chives

The trick here is to wok-char the cauliflower to bring out its smoky, sweet flavours. Then, with the spicy, savoury hoisin sauce, the pungent chives and the crunchy pine nuts, it's a deeply satisfying dish – perfect with noodles or rice or even on its own.

Serves 2 kcal 310 carbs 30g protein 10.1g fat 17.3g

Whisk together all the ingredients for the sauce in a small jug, then set aside.

Heat a wok over a high heat until smoking and add the rapeseed oil. Add the cauliflower florets and stir-fry for 30 seconds, then drizzle in 30ml cold water around the edge of the wok to create some steam to help cook the florets. Keep stirring until any liquid evaporates, charring the florets.

Pour in the sauce and stir carefully to coat the florets well. Bring the sauce to the boil and cook until glossy and the cauliflower is tender, about 4 minutes.

Finally, garnish with the pine nuts and chopped chives and serve.

V Ve GF DF

Spicy Soy Mushroom Tofu

1 tablespoon rapeseed oil

2 garlic cloves, finely chopped

knob of fresh root ginger, peeled and finely grated

400g fresh firm tofu, drained and sliced into 2cm cubes

1 tablespoon Shaohsing rice wine or dry sherry

2 tablespoons tamari

1 tablespoon mushroom 'oyster' sauce

1 teaspoon sriracha chilli sauce

1 tablespoon clear rice vinegar or cider vinegar

For the garnish

10g chopped chives

1 teaspoon shichimi pepper flakes

Tofu can be boring but here it is enhanced by many layers of Chinese flavours – bittersweet Shaohsing rice wine, umami tamari, rich, earthy mushroom sauce and tangy sriracha heat – which all combine to make this a true vegan winner. It's perfect on a veggie bibimbap (a Korean rice dish) or with plain rice and pickles on the side.

Serves 2 kcal 258 carbs 9.3g protein 21.4g fat 14.3g

Heat a wok over a high heat and, as the wok starts to smoke, add the rapeseed oil. Add the garlic and ginger and fry for a few seconds, then add the tofu cubes. Stir-fry for 1 minute to brown, then add the Shaohsing rice wine or dry sherry.

Season with the tamari, mushroom 'oyster' sauce, sriracha and vinegar and gently toss, then flip the tofu over, being careful not to break up the pieces, and cook for 1 minute.

Garnish with the chopped chives and shichimi pepper and serve.

20
mins*

5
mins

*includes cooking the rice

V Ve DF

Shiitake, Kimchi and Pineapple Fried Rice

1 tablespoon rapeseed oil
knob of fresh root ginger,
    peeled and grated
5 large fresh shiitake mushrooms,
    rinsed, patted dry and cut into
    thin slices, stalks optional
½ teaspoon dark soy sauce
1 tablespoon fermented
    cucumber kimchi, finely sliced
300g cooked brown rice (150g
    uncooked)
2 tablespoons low-sodium light
    soy sauce
100g fresh pineapple, finely
    diced into cubes
5g spring onions, sliced on
    a deep diagonal, to garnish

A delicious sweet, umami-flavoured fried rice. Perfect for supper, any night of the week.

Serves 2 kcal 291 carbs 51.8g protein 7.4g fat 7.3g

Heat a wok over a high heat until smoking and add the rapeseed oil. Add the grated ginger and stir-fry for 5 seconds, then add the shiitake mushrooms and stir-fry for 30 seconds.

Season with the dark soy sauce, then add the sliced cucumber kimchi followed by the cooked rice and toss together for 1 minute.

Season with the light soy sauce, then add the fresh pineapple cubes and toss gently into the rice. Garnish with the spring onions and serve immediately.

V Ve DF

Wok-fried Radicchio with Jicama, Blood Orange, Pomelo and Cashew Nuts

1 tablespoon rapeseed oil

1 garlic clove, finely chopped

300g radicchio, washed and torn into bite-size pieces

1 teaspoon fried garlic and shallots (see page 22)

1 teaspoon low-sodium light soy sauce

For the garnish

50g peeled and grated jicama

1 ripe blood orange, peeled and segmented

¼ pomelo or grapefruit, finely sliced

1 small handful of roasted salted cashew nuts

zest and juice of 1 lime

A fresh and zingy wok-cooked dish, perfect for hot summer days. Sear the radicchio over a high heat for a charred smoky flavour and if you can't get jicama, use grated crunchy apples or pears instead.

Serves 2 kcal 197 carbs 18.7g protein 4.6g fat 13.2g

Heat a wok over a high heat and, as the wok starts to smoke, add the rapeseed oil and garlic and stir-fry for 5 seconds. Add the radicchio and toss for 5 seconds until slightly charred and wilted, then toss in the garlic-fried shallots and add the light soy sauce. Transfer to a serving plate.

Garnish with the grated jicama, blood orange segments, pomelo or grapefruit slices and cashew nuts. Sprinkle with the lime zest and squeeze the lime juice over. Serve immediately.

10 mins*

12 mins

*includes cooking
the noodles

V   DF

Vegetarian Hokkien Mee

1 tablespoon rapeseed oil
2 garlic cloves, finely chopped
knob of fresh root ginger,
    peeled and grated
2 mini sweet shallots, finely
    chopped
1 red chilli, deseeded and finely
    chopped
3 dried Chinese mushrooms,
    soaked in warm water for
    20 minutes, drained and stalks
    discarded, finely diced
100g Quorn mince or
    minced soy protein
1 teaspoon dark soy sauce
100ml hot vegetable stock
1 tablespoon low-sodium light
    soy sauce
drizzle of toasted sesame oil
400g cooked egg noodles
    (200g dried)
100g fresh beansprouts,
    blanched in boiling water for
    10 seconds, rinsed in cold
    water and drained

For the garnish
red chilli, thinly sliced into rings
    (optional)
a few spring onions, or chives,
    sliced on the diagonal

Hokkien Mee is a Malaysian Chinese dish that is usually topped with pork and shrimp and served on egg noodles. My vegetarian version swaps the meat and shellfish for braised Chinese mushrooms and minced soy protein and, in my opinion, they provide a rich, savoury topping that is just as good. It's delicious garnished with spring onion, which adds a fresh bite, and a little red chilli for an extra kick.

Serves 2 kcal 493 carbs 66.5g protein 20.2g fat 16.2g

Heat a wok over a high heat and add the rapeseed oil. Add the garlic, ginger, shallots and chilli and explode the flavours in the wok for a few seconds. Add the diced Chinese mushrooms and the Quorn mince or minced soy protein and season with the dark soy sauce to enrich the colour. Add the vegetable stock and light soy sauce and leave to cook for 10 minutes until the sauce has reduced.

Meanwhile, drizzle some toasted sesame oil over the cooked egg noodles. Divide the noodles between two bowls, top with the braised soy mushrooms Quorn mince and garnish with beansprouts, fresh chillies and sliced spring onions. Serve immediately.

20 mins*

7 mins

* includes soaking the mushrooms

V Ve DF

Hot and Sour Chinese Cabbage

1 tablespoon rapeseed oil

knob of fresh root ginger, peeled and grated

1 red chilli, deseeded and finely chopped

20g wood ear mushrooms, soaked in hot water for 20 minutes, then drained and sliced into thin strips

300g Chinese leaf or Chinese napa cabbage, stalks removed and cut into 2.5cm slices

1 tablespoon Shaohsing rice wine or dry sherry

100ml vegetable stock

1 tablespoon low-sodium light soy sauce

½ teaspoon dark soy sauce

1 tablespoon clear rice vinegar or cider vinegar

1 tablespoon cornflour blended with 2 tablespoons cold water

2 spring onions, sliced into julienne strips

This is a beautifully warming winter dish, perfect served with rice or poured on top of thin wheat-flour noodles. The spicy hot and sour notes of the dish make it incredibly flavoursome and moreish.

Serves 2 kcal 150 carbs 20.6g protein 3.2g fat 6.4g

Heat a wok over a high heat and, as the wok starts to smoke, add the rapeseed oil. Add the ginger and chilli and stir-fry for a few seconds, then add the wood ear mushrooms and Chinese leaves or cabbage and toss for 1 minute. Drizzle 30ml cold water around the edge of the wok to create some steam to help cook the vegetables.

Add the Shaohsing rice wine or dry sherry, then pour in the vegetable stock and season with the light and dark soy sauces and the vinegar. Bring to the boil, then add the blended cornflour and stir to thicken.

Garnish with the sliced spring onion and serve immediately.

V Ve DF

Sichuan Smoked Tofu Gan with Celery and Roasted Peanuts

1 tablespoon rapeseed oil

1 garlic clove, minced

1 teaspoon ground dry-toasted
    Sichuan peppercorns

Chinese celery sticks and leaves,
    or celery, cut on the diagonal
    into 5mm-thick slices

200g piece of firm tofu gan
    (dried firm smoked bean curd),
    cut into 3mm-thick slices

1 teaspoon chilli bean paste

1 tablespoon Chinkiang black
    rice vinegar or balsamic
    vinegar

1 tablespoon low-sodium light
    soy sauce

1 tablespoon chilli oil

pinch of freshly ground white
    pepper

juice of ½ lemon

For the garnish

small handful of roasted
    peanuts, crushed

small handful of fresh coriander,
    finely chopped

This dish delivers a deliciously spicy vegan hit that is perfect served with boiled rice and a scattering of crunchy peanuts.

Serves 2 kcal 351 carbs 7.6g protein 20.8g fat 26.4g

Heat a wok over a high heat and, as the wok starts to smoke, add the rapeseed oil. Add the garlic and ground Sichuan peppercorns and stir-fry for 5 seconds. Add the celery and stir-fry for 1 minute until softened, then add the tofu slices and carefully toss until heated through – about 1 minute.

Add the chilli bean paste and Chinkiang rice vinegar and toss. Season with the light soy sauce, plus the chilli oil, ground white pepper and a squeeze of lemon juice and toss again.

Transfer to a serving plate and sprinkle with the crushed peanuts and chopped coriander. Serve immediately.

V · Ve · DF

Tofu, Tomato, Mushroom and Spring Onion Scramble

1 tablespoon rapeseed oil

2 large ripe tomatoes, each cored and cut into 6 wedges

100g shimeji mushrooms

1 tablespoon Shaohsing rice wine or dry sherry

250g fresh firm tofu, drained and very lightly broken up using a fork

pinch of ground turmeric

pinch of dried chilli flakes

1 tablespoon low-sodium light soy sauce

pinch of sea salt flakes

pinch of ground black pepper

1 spring onion, sliced on the diagonal, to garnish

This is a real home-style dish and reminds me of my grandmother's cooking. It's a bit like making scrambled eggs but using tofu as the star. This scramble is vegan friendly and should be light and fluffy; it's delicious served with boiled rice.

Serves 2 kcal 191 carbs 8.4g protein 13.7g fat 11.2g

Heat a wok over a high heat and add the rapeseed oil. When the oil starts to smoke, add the tomatoes and stir-fry for 1 minute until softened. Add the shimeji mushrooms and stir-fry for 1 minute until browned. Season with the Shaohsing rice wine or dry sherry. Add the tofu and stir in to mix well. Season with the turmeric and dried chilli flakes and cook for 1 minute. Add the light soy sauce and toss, cooking until all the soy has covered the tofu, then season with salt and black pepper.

Garnish with the spring onion and serve immediately.

20 mins*

4 mins

* includes chilling time

V Ve DF

Sichuan French Beans on Chilled Silken Tofu

1 tablespoon rapeseed oil

knob of fresh root ginger, peeled and grated

1 teaspoon ground dry-toasted Sichuan peppercorns

1 medium red chilli, deseeded and finely chopped

200g French beans, sliced into 5mm rounds

1 tablespoon lemon juice

1 tablespoon clear rice vinegar or cider vinegar

1 tablespoon low-sodium light soy sauce

1 tablespoon chilli oil

1 teaspoon toasted sesame oil

400g ready-to-eat, firm silken tofu, drained and sliced into 1cm cubes, chilled for 20 minutes and served as one block

small handful of fresh coriander stems and leaves, finely chopped, to garnish

This is a great way to cook French beans but it is important they are fresh. When you buy them, snap one in half and, if it makes a crunchy snap, you know they are at their best. This dish is very quick to prepare and the contrast between the hot, spicy beans and the chilled, silken tofu is delicious. Serve with steamed rice or enjoy simply on its own.

Serves 2 kcal 276 carbs 9.1g protein 17.1g fat 18.5g

Heat a wok over a high heat and, as the woke starts to smoke, add the rapeseed oil. Add the ginger, Sichuan pepper and red chilli and toss for a few seconds.

Add the French beans and toss well, then add a small splash of cold water to create some steam to help cook the beans. Toss for 2–3 minutes until the beans are tender, then season with the lemon juice, vinegar, light soy sauce and the chilli and toasted sesame oils and take off the heat.

Place the chilled silken tofu in a bowl. Pour the beans over, garnish with the chopped coriander leaves and stems and serve immediately.

5 mins

8 mins

V Ve DF

Edamame Mapo Tofu

1 tablespoon rapeseed oil

2 garlic cloves, crushed and
finely chopped

1 tablespoon fresh root ginger,
peeled and grated

1 medium red chilli, deseeded
and finely chopped

200g edamame beans

400g fresh firm tofu, drained
and cut into 2.5cm chunks

2 tablespoons chilli bean paste

1 tablespoon Shaohsing rice
wine or dry sherry

pinch of sea salt flakes

pinch of ground white pepper

pinch of ground dry-toasted
Sichuan peppercorns

2 large spring onions, cut into
julienne slices and soaked
in iced water to curl

For the sauce

200ml cold vegetable stock

1 tablespoon Chinkiang black
rice vinegar or balsamic
vinegar

1 teaspoon low-sodium light
soy sauce

1 tablespoon cornflour

Mapo tofu is a Sichuanese dish named after a famous Sichuan vendor who was recognised by her pockmarked appearance – this dish is traditionally also known as 'Mrs. Pockmarked Tofu'. The classic version uses minced pork and sometimes minced beef. However, I like to use edamame beans instead, which add a satisfying bite in contrast to the soft tofu. This is a delicious recipe through and through and is great served with plain boiled rice to soak up the spicy sauce.

Serves 2 kcal 467 carbs 27.4g protein 33.2g fat 23.4g

Whisk together all the ingredients for the sauce in a bowl, then set aside.

Heat a wok over a high heat and, as the wok starts to smoke, add the rapeseed oil. Add the garlic, ginger and chopped chilli and stir-fry to explode the flavours. Add the edamame and stir-fry for a few seconds, then add the tofu and toss, cooking for a few more seconds.

Add the chilli bean paste and the Shaohsing rice wine and cook for 1 minute, then add the sauce. Bring to the boil and cook until thickened. Season further to taste with the salt, ground white pepper and ground Sichuan peppercorns, then stir and add the spring onions. Serve immediately.

Kung Po Tofu

1 tablespoon rapeseed oil

1 tablespoon Sichuan peppercorns

3 whole dried chillies

200g fried tofu, cut into 2cm cubes

1 tablespoon Shaohsing rice wine or dry sherry

1 small red pepper, deseeded and chopped into small chunks

handful of dry roasted peanuts or cashew nuts

2 spring onions, sliced on the diagonal

For the sauce

100ml cold vegetable stock

1 tablespoon low-sodium light soy sauce

1 tablespoon ketchup

1 tablespoon Chinkiang black rice vinegar or balsamic vinegar

1 teaspoon sriracha chilli sauce or good chilli sauce

1 tablespoon cornflour

This is a great Sichuan dish that was invented by Ding Baozhen, the dearly loved governor of Sichuan in the nineteenth century. Its numbing, spicy sweet and tangy flavours are delicious with crispy fried tofu or, if you like meat, fry seasoned chicken strips first, then follow the rest of the steps. Also, if you'd prefer a healthier alternative to fried tofu, use smoked firm tofu instead.

Serves 2 kcal 470 carbs 23g protein 28.9g fat 30.3g

Whisk together all the ingredients for the sauce in a small glass jug, then set aside.

Heat a wok over a high heat until smoking and add the rapeseed oil. Add the Sichuan peppercorns and dried chillies and stir-fry for a few seconds, then add the tofu cubes and stir-fry for 1 minute until the tofu is seared at the edges. Add the Shaohsing rice wine or dry sherry, then the red pepper and cook for just under 30 seconds.

Give the sauce a quick stir, then pour into the wok and bring to the boil. When the sauce has reduced and is thicker and slightly sticky, add the peanuts or cashew nuts, followed by the spring onions and cook for 1 minute. Stir to mix everything together well, then transfer to a serving plate and serve immediately.

* includes soaking the mushrooms

V Ve DF

Black Bean Buddha's Stir-fried Mixed Vegetables

1 tablespoon rapeseed oil

knob of fresh root ginger, peeled and grated

½ teaspoon fermented salted black beans, rinsed, then crushed with 1 tablespoon Shaohsing rice wine or dry sherry

1 medium carrot, cut into julienne strips

4 fresh shiitake mushrooms, rinsed, dried and sliced

small handful of dried wood ear mushrooms, soaked in hot water for 20 minutes, drained and sliced into 1cm strips

small handful of baby sweetcorn, sliced in half on the diagonal

1 x 225g can of bamboo shoots, drained and cut into julienne strips

a small handful of fresh beansprouts

2 spring onions, finely sliced, to garnish

For the sauce

100ml cold vegetable stock

1 tablespoon low-sodium light soy sauce

1 tablespoon vegetarian mushroom sauce

1 teaspoon toasted sesame oil

1 tablespoon cornflour

Buddha's Stir-fried Mixed Vegetables is a famous Chinese dish that is served at all important festivals throughout the year. Typically, a dish such as this would contain straw mushrooms and dried lily flowers. However, you can use a bag of mixed stir-fry vegetables – beansprouts, cabbage, peppers and onions, or any assorted vegetable medley that you prefer. I'm adding fermented salted black beans, and in my opinion, Chinese wood ear mushrooms, although bland in taste, provide excellent textural crunch. Both these ingredients can be bought from a Chinese supermarket or online and I promise they'll soon become your store cupboard stir-fry staples.

Serves 2 kcal 206 carbs 25.6g protein 5.4g fat 9.2g

Whisk together all the ingredients for the sauce in a small jug, then set aside.

Heat a wok over a high heat and, as the wok starts to smoke, add the rapeseed oil. Add the ginger and stir-fry for a few seconds, then add the fermented salted black bean mixture and toss for 2 seconds. Next, add the carrot and cook for 1 minute, then the shiitake mushrooms, wood ear mushrooms, baby corn and bamboo shoots and stir-fry together for 1 minute.

Add the sauce and bring to the boil. When the sauce has thickened, add the beansprouts and cook for 30 seconds, then garnish with the spring onions. Transfer to a serving plate and serve immediately.

Yellow Bean Sesame Beansprouts

1 tablespoon rapeseed oil

1 teaspoon freshly grated root ginger

3 spring onions, trimmed and finely sliced into rounds

500g fresh beansprouts

1 teaspoon toasted white sesame seeds, to garnish

For the sauce

1 teaspoon Shaohsing rice wine or dry sherry

1 teaspoon whole fermented yellow beans

1 tablespoon vegetarian mushroom sauce

1 tablespoon low-sodium light soy sauce

50ml cold vegetable stock

1 teaspoon cornflour

This dish is quick and simple but full of flavour. The punchy fermented yellow beans transform the beansprouts and the sesame seeds and spring onion round it off nicely with a fresh, nutty, aromatic bite. It's great with meat and fish dishes and also alongside stir-fried vegetables. Sometimes simplicity is king.

Serves 4 kcal 106 carbs 7.3g protein 3.9g fat 6.4g

Whisk together all the ingredients for the sauce in a small jug, then set aside.

Heat a wok over a high heat and, as the wok starts to smoke, add the rapeseed oil. Add the ginger and stir-fry for a few seconds, then add the spring onions and toss for 5 seconds. Add the beansprouts, then pour in the sauce and toss on a high heat for 30 seconds, ensuring that the sauce coats the beansprouts well.

Transfer to a serving plate, garnish with the toasted sesame seeds and serve immediately.

20 mins*

6-7 mins

* includes cooking the rice

V Ve DF

1 tablespoon rapeseed oil

knob of fresh root ginger, peeled and grated

1 red cayenne chilli, deseeded and finely chopped

2 spring onions, trimmed and sliced into 1cm rounds

¼ teaspoon medium curry powder

200g courgettes, halved lengthways, then cut into 5mm half-moon slices

1 tablespoon Shaohsing rice wine or dry sherry

150g lotus root, blanched in hot water, drained and cut into 5mm slices

300g cooked basmati rice (150g uncooked)

2 tablespoons low-sodium light soy sauce

1 teaspoon toasted sesame oil

2 pinches of cracked black pepper

Curried Courgette and Lotus Root Fried Rice

I love this combination of sweet courgettes and crunchy lotus roots. If you can't get lotus root, substitute canned water chestnuts – they work just as well. Satisfying, tasty and healthy!

Serves 2 kcal 314 carbs 52.9g protein 8.9g fat 8.8g

Heat a wok over a high heat and, as the wok begins to smoke, add the rapeseed oil. Add the ginger, chopped chilli and spring onions and explode the flavours in the wok for a few seconds.

Add the curry powder followed by the courgettes, then toss for 30 seconds and season with the Shaohsing rice wine or dry sherry. Add the lotus root pieces and toss for 30 seconds, then add the cooked rice and toss for 3 minutes so that all the flavours are incorporated.

Season with the light soy sauce, toasted sesame oil and cracked black pepper and serve.

Spicy Saucy Sichuan Mushroom Chow Mein

V DF

1 tablespoon rapeseed oil

2 small garlic cloves, crushed
and roughly chopped

2.5cm piece of fresh root ginger,
peeled and finely grated

1 large red cayenne chilli,
deseeded and sliced

200g oyster mushrooms

120g baby pak choy, leaves
separated

1 tablespoon Shaohsing rice
wine or dry sherry

300g cooked egg noodles (150g
uncooked)

For the Sichuan spicy sauce

100ml cold water

1 tablespoon chilli bean paste

2 tablespoons Chinkiang black
rice vinegar or balsamic
vinegar

1 tablespoon low-sodium light
soy sauce

1 teaspoon soft brown sugar

1 tablespoon cornflour

1 teaspoon toasted sesame oil

A quick mid-week supper that's delicious, simple and packs a punch. I love using oyster mushrooms, but you can use whatever mushrooms you prefer.

Serves 2 kcal 404 carbs 62.8g protein 11g fat 12.6g

Whisk together all the ingredients for the Sichuan spicy sauce in a small jug or bowl, then set aside.

Heat a wok over a high heat until smoking, then add the rapeseed oil. Add the garlic, ginger and chilli and stir-fry for a few seconds. Add the mushrooms and cook for 1 minute, then add the pak choy leaves and Shaohsing rice wine or dry sherry and toss for 1 minute.

Add the spicy sauce and bring to the boil. Add the cooked egg noodles and toss together until the sauce coats all the noodles and the noodles are warmed through. Serve immediately.

10 mins*

5 mins

* includes cooking the noodles

V DF

Hoisin Mangetout and Cashew Nut Chow Mein

1 tablespoon rapeseed oil

knob of fresh root ginger, peeled and grated

150g mangetout, sliced in half if large

150g sugarsnap peas

pinch of Chinese five-spice powder

50ml cold vegetable stock

1 tablespoon hoisin sauce

2 tablespoons low-sodium light soy sauce

pinch of soft brown sugar

2 tablespoons roasted cashew nuts

For the noodles

300g cooked egg noodles (150g dried noodles)

1 teaspoon toasted sesame oil

Here the crunchy mangetout, sugarsnap peas and cashew nuts contrast beautifully with the soft egg noodles. Perfect for a quick mid-week supper.

Serves 2 kcal 444 carbs 58.4g protein 15.5g fat 17.4g

If using dried noodles, cook according to the packet instructions. Drain and refresh under cold water, then drizzle with the toasted sesame oil and set aside.

Heat a wok over a high heat until smoking and add the rapeseed oil. Add the ginger and stir-fry for 5 seconds, then add the mangetout and sugarsnap peas. Toss for 1 minute, then season with a pinch of five-spice powder.

Add the vegetable stock, followed by the cooked noodles and toss for 1 minute. Season with the hoisin, light soy sauce and soft brown sugar, then add the cashew nuts and toss together for 1 minute.

Transfer to a serving plate and serve immediately.

V Ve DF

Vegetable Chop Suey

1 tablespoon rapeseed oil
2 garlic cloves, finely chopped
1/2 white onion, cut into
    half-moon slices
1 medium carrot, cut into
    2.5 x 1cm rectangular slices
4 large fresh shiitake
    mushrooms, sliced
150g tenderstem broccoli,
    sliced on the diagonal into
    2.5cm pieces
1 tablespoon Shaohsing rice
    wine or dry sherry
1 x 225g can water chestnuts,
    drained
large handful of beansprouts
2 spring onions, trimmed and cut
    on the angle into 2.5cm slices

For the sauce
100ml cold vegetable stock
1 tablespoon low-sodium light
    soy sauce
1 teaspoon rice vinegar
pinch of soft brown sugar
1 tablespoon cornflour

In Chinese, this dish is called 'Za Tsui', which means 'chopped pieces', which can mean vegetables as well as slivers of prawns, pork, chicken or tofu and is often made up of leftovers. Essentially, anything goes. It dates from the time of the American Gold Rush when Chinese immigrants, brought over to work on the American railroad, would cook whatever was available, often together with Egg Foo Yung (see page 101). It's humble but so satisfying that it is still popular to this day. Serve with steamed jasmine rice or you can toss in cooked egg noodles for a saucy chow mein.

Serves 2 kcal 197 carbs 25.7g protein 6.8g fat 8g

Whisk together all the ingredients for the sauce in a jug, then set aside.

Heat a wok over a high heat until smoking and add the rapeseed oil. Add the garlic and white onion and stir-fry for 10 seconds to release their aroma. Add the carrot and toss for 2 minutes until softened, then add the shiitake mushrooms and broccoli and toss on a high heat for 30 seconds.

Season with the Shaohsing rice wine or dry sherry, then add the water chestnuts, beansprouts and spring onions. Pour in the sauce and bring to the boil, coating the ingredients well.

Immediately transfer to a serving dish and serve.

15 mins*

5-6 mins

* includes soaking time

V DF

1 tablespoon rapeseed oil
pinch of sea salt flakes
1 tablespoon freshly grated
    root ginger
3 garlic cloves, finely chopped
200g asparagus spears, cut into
    5cm slices
1 tablespoon Shaohsing rice
    wine or dry sherry
30g dried wood ear mushrooms,
    soaked in hot water for
    15 minutes, drained and cut
    into 2.5cm 'wavy' pieces
50ml vegetable stock
1 tablespoon potato flour
    blended with 1 tablespoon
    cold water
1 teaspoon low-sodium light
    soy sauce
½ teaspoon toasted sesame oil
small handful of roasted
    cashew nuts
300g cooked egg noodles
    (150g uncooked)
1 teaspoon toasted sesame oil

Asparagus, Wood Ear Mushrooms and Cashew Nuts in Ginger Garlic Sauce

This makes a delicious meal in minutes – nothing beats fresh asparagus in a sticky, saucy stir-fry. However, be prepared to move fast and read the recipe through prior to cooking so the process is in your head before you start. You won't have time to stop and chop, let alone stop and read. And don't forget to finish with a crunch of your choice, I love roasted cashew nuts.

Serves 2 kcal 495 carbs 66.7g protein 14.1g fat 19.7g

Cook the noodles according to the packet instructions, then rinse under the cold tap, drain and drizzle with the sesame oil.

Heat a wok over a high heat until smoking, then add the rapeseed oil and give the oil a swirl. Add the sea salt and let it dissolve in the hot oil. Add the ginger and garlic in quick succession and stir-fry for a few seconds, then add the asparagus and stir-fry for less than 1 minute. Add the Shaohsing rice wine around the rim of the wok to create steam and cook until it has all evaporated.

Add the wood ear mushrooms and toss together for another minute, then add the vegetable stock. Bring the liquid to the boil, then stir in the blended potato flour – this helps bind the sauce to the ingredients. Season with the soy sauce and add a drop of sesame oil, then toss in the cashew nuts – all in one swoop. Add the cooked egg noodles and toss for 30 seconds to heat through. Give everything a final stir then serve.

> CHING'S TIP
> Please read the recipe through prior to cooking so the process is in your head before you start, as you won't have time to stop and chop, or even stop and read.
> Keep the wok on the highest heat at all times; if it gets too hot, move it away from the heat source. If it's not hot enough, bring it back to the heat. If ingredients start to burn, add a small splash of water to reduce the heat and prevent them from burning further.

V DF

Vegetarian Tofu-style Lionhead 'Meatballs'

500ml peanut oil
750ml vegetable stock
100g Chinese leaf, sliced
lengthways into 3cm wide
strips
3 fresh shiitake mushrooms,
sliced
100g mung bean noodles
1 tablespoon low-sodium light
soy sauce
pinch of salt
pinch of ground white pepper
1 tablespoon cornflour blended
with 2 tablespoons cold water
(optional)
2 large spring onions, trimmed
and cut on a deep diagonal
into 2cm pieces

For the 'meatballs'
300g fresh firm tofu, drained
1 teaspoon freshly grated
root ginger
5g fresh coriander stems, finely
chopped
1 spring onion, finely chopped
1 teaspoon Shaohsing rice
wine or dry sherry
1/2 teaspoon toasted sesame oil
pinch of sea salt flakes
pinch of ground white pepper
1 medium egg, lightly beaten
50g cornflour

Lionhead Meatballs is a dish that originates from Shanghai and is said to have been something the emperor ate. The meatballs are usually made of pork and first deep-fried, then braised and served in a light broth of Chinese leaves, curled around each meatball to resemble the 'mane' of a lion. For my vegetarian version I've substituted mashed tofu for pork mince, but the seasoning ingredients are the same as for the traditional meatballs. You can serve them in broth, with rice or add mung bean noodles, as I have here.

Serves 2 kcal 665 carbs 85.8g protein 21g fat 27.9g

First make the 'meatballs'. Put the tofu in a large bowl and mash with a fork. Add all the remaining 'meatball' ingredients except the cornflour and stir to combine. Using wetted hands, shape the mixture into 12 medium golf ball shapes, then dust with the cornflour and place on a plate.

Heat a wok over a high heat until smoking and add the peanut oil. Using a spider or metal spoon, carefully lower each meatball into the oil and spoon some of the oil over the meatballs to brown them. When the meatballs have turned golden brown, remove carefully and place on a heatproof plate lined with paper towels. For a crisper meatball, you can deep-fry them twice by reheating the oil and repeating the process.

Leave 1 tablespoon of oil in the wok and pour the rest into a heatproof bowl. Add the stock, Chinese leaf, mushrooms, mung bean noodles and soy sauce and bring to the boil. Cook on a medium heat for 6–7 minutes until the noodles are cooked through and translucent and the Chinese leaf has wilted, then season to taste with salt and white pepper and stir in the blended cornflour (this adds a silky texture to the broth).

Ladle the broth and noodles into a serving bowl, add the tofu balls and sprinkle with the spring onions. Serve immediately.

Honey Miso Broccoli and Cauliflower

V DF

1 tablespoon rapeseed oil

1 small spring onion, sliced

150g broccoli, separated into florets, stalks cut on the diagonal into 5mm slices

150g cauliflower, separated into florets, stalks cut on the diagonal into 5mm slices

toasted pumpkin seeds (optional), to garnish

For the sauce

1 tablespoon red miso paste

1 teaspoon peeled and grated fresh root ginger

1 tablespoon runny honey

pinch of shichimi pepper flakes (optional)

1 tablespoon tamari

3 tablespoons mirin

I love the sweet salty combination of honey and miso; it's delicious with vegetables and even popular with children who think they don't like broccoli. Easy and simple and extremely healthy when served like this with pumpkin seeds and brown rice.

Serves 2 kcal 223 carbs 26.9g protein 7.9g fat 9.1g

Whisk together all the ingredients for the sauce in a jug, then set aside.

Heat a wok over a high heat and, as the wok starts to smoke, add the rapeseed oil. Add the spring onion and stir-fry for a few seconds to release its aroma, then add the broccoli and cauliflower and toss for 1 minute. Drizzle in 50ml cold water around the edge of the wok to create some steam to help cook the vegetables.

Give the sauce a stir, then add to the wok and toss everything together on a high heat, ensuring all the vegetables are coated in the sauce. Cook for 1 minute.

Garnish with the pumpkin seeds (if using) and transfer to a serving plate.

V Ve DF

Sweetheart Cabbage with Sweetcorn and Chilli

2 tablespoons rapeseed oil

2 garlic cloves, crushed and finely chopped

2.5cm piece of fresh root ginger, peeled and grated

1 small cayenne chilli, deseeded and finely chopped

300g sweetheart cabbage leaves, sliced into 2.5cm pieces

kernels from 2 whole fresh sweetcorn

2 tablespoons Shaohsing rice wine or dry sherry

50ml vegetable stock

2 tablespoons low-sodium light soy sauce

1 teaspoon cornflour blended with 1 tablespoon cold water

1 teaspoon toasted sesame oil

1 large spring onion, finely sliced (optional), to garnish

The hot chilli and umami soy perfectly balance out the sweetness of the cabbage leaves and crunchy corn kernels. Perfect with steamed rice for a light, healthy supper.

Serves 2 kcal 263 carbs 23.3g protein 9.2g fat 15.4g

Heat a wok over a high heat until smoking and add the rapeseed oil. Swirl the oil in the pan, then add the garlic, ginger and cayenne chilli and stir-fry very quickly for a few seconds. Add the cabbage leaves and cook for 1 minute, tossing them in the wok until seared and starting to wilt. Add the corn kernels and toss for 1 minute, then season with the Shaohsing rice wine or dry sherry and cook until evaporated.

Add the vegetable stock and season with the light soy sauce, then bring any liquid in the wok to a simmer. Pour in the blended cornflour and toss to mix well, then season with the toasted sesame oil.

Garnish with the spring onion and serve immediately.

General Tso's Tofu

400g fresh firm tofu, drained
  and cut into 2.5cm cubes
60g potato flour or cornflour
groundnut oil, for deep-frying
1 egg, lightly beaten
1 garlic clove, crushed but
  left whole
4 whole dried Sichuan chillies
1 medium white onion, cut into
  2.5cm squares
1 large red pepper, deseeded
  and cut into 2.5cm squares
1 tablespoon Shaohsing rice
  wine or dry sherry
4 spring onions, chopped into
  2.5cm pieces

For the sauce
1 tablespoon yellow bean sauce
2 tablespoons low-sodium light
  soy sauce
1 tablespoon tomato paste
1 tablespoon clear rice vinegar
  or cider vinegar
1 tablespoon chilli sauce
1 teaspoon light brown sugar
  or honey
1 teaspoon dark soy sauce

For the garnish and to serve
80g peanuts, toasted and
  chopped (optional)
handful of toasted sesame seeds

Variations of this recipe are found all over the world. It was invented by a Hunanese chef named Peng-Chang Kuei, who cooked at state banquets and official events for the Chinese Nationalist party and fled with them to Taiwan during the Second World War, where he came up with the dish in the 1950s. Its original flavours were Hunanese – hot, sour, salty and heavy – but when he moved to New York in 1973 he made it sweeter to suit the American palate. The original dish used chicken but I like it with crunchy fried tofu. If you don't like frying the tofu, use smoked firm tofu and follow the rest of the recipe. Serve with steamed jasmine rice and broccoli.

Serves 2 kcal 915 carbs 52.9g protein 37.5g fat 61.9g

Whisk together all the ingredients for the sauce in a bowl, then set aside.

Next, coat the tofu cubes in the potato flour or cornflour and place on a plate. Heat a wok over a high heat until smoking and fill to a quarter of its depth with groundnut oil. Heat the oil to 180°C or until a piece of bread dropped in turns golden brown in 15 seconds. Coat each piece of tofu in the beaten egg and, using a spider or slotted metal spoon, lower into the wok. Cook for about 5 minutes until all the tofu is golden brown, then remove and place on a plate lined with kitchen paper to drain any excess oil.

Leave 1 tablespoon oil in the wok and strain the rest through a sieve into a heatproof bowl. Heat the wok over a high heat and, when it starts to smoke, add the garlic and dried chillies and fry for a few seconds to release their aroma. Add the white onion and stir-fry for 1 minute, then add the red pepper and Shaohsing rice wine or dry sherry and cook until the sauce has reduced and has a slightly sticky consistency. Toss in the fried tofu pieces and add the spring onions.

Transfer to a serving plate and garnish with the peanuts and sesame seeds.

* includes marinating
the mock duck

(V) (Ve) (DF)

Five-spice Mock Duck and Seasonal Greens

300g canned mock duck,
    drained and cut into 1cm strips
1 tablespoon rapeseed oil
2 whole dried chillies, torn
1 tablespoon Shaohsing rice
    wine or dry sherry
50g tenderstem broccoli,
    sliced on the diagonal into
    2.5cm pieces
50g French beans, sliced on the
    diagonal into 2.5cm pieces
1 tablespoon cornflour blended
    with 2 tablespoons cold water
1 spring onion, finely sliced, to
    garnish

For the marinade
1 garlic clove, finely chopped
1 teaspoon Chinese five-spice
    powder
1 teaspoon dark soy sauce
pinch of sea salt flakes
pinch of ground white pepper

Mock duck is made from wheat gluten and gives a meaty texture, 'mocking' meat. It is used in a lot of Buddhist vegetarian dishes within Chinese cuisine and it comes in cans which can be found in most Chinese supermarkets. If you can't get it, use meaty portobello mushrooms or smoked tofu. For meat lovers, a tender sirloin steak or chicken thighs sliced into strips work well – just dust the strips with cornflour after marinating to seal in the meat juices before frying. Enjoy!

Serves 2 kcal 253 carbs 18.9g protein 21.1g fat 11.1g

Place all the ingredients for the marinade in a small bowl or plastic bag, add the mock duck and marinate for 20 minutes.

Heat a wok over a high heat until smoking and add the rapeseed oil. Add the dried chillies and toss for 10 seconds to release their aroma, then add the marinated mock duck pieces and toss for 30 seconds. Season with the Shaohsing rice wine or dry sherry and cook until evaporated.

Add the broccoli and French beans and toss for 1 minute until tender and the vegetables turn a deeper opaque green. Add 100ml cold water and bring to a simmer, then stir in the blended cornflour to thicken the sauce. Garnish with the spring onion and serve immediately.

King Trumpet Mushrooms with Chives

V Ve DF

1 tablespoon rapeseed oil

knob of fresh root ginger, peeled and grated

300g King Trumpet mushrooms, cut into 1cm slices

1–2 tablespoons Shaohsing rice wine or dry sherry

1 tablespoon mushroom 'oyster' sauce

1 tablespoon low-sodium light soy sauce

pinch of ground black pepper

5g chives, finely chopped, to garnish

If you are a fan of Beef in Oyster Sauce but looking for a veggie alternative, then this is the dish for you. King Trumpet mushrooms are meaty in texture and the perfect accompaniment to a rich oyster sauce. This is simple, easy and delicious. Perfect served with steamed seasonal greens and some steamed jasmine rice.

Serves 2 kcal 76 carbs 3.4g protein 2.3g fat 5.9g

Heat a wok over a high heat until smoking and add the rapeseed oil. Add the ginger and stir-fry for a few seconds to release its aroma, then add the King Trumpet pieces and sear for 30 seconds.

Add the Shaohsing rice wine or dry sherry and cook until evaporated. Season with the oyster or mushroom sauce, the light soy sauce and a pinch of ground black pepper.

Garnish with the chopped chives and serve immediately.

V Ve DF

Aubergines in a Spicy Peanut Sauce

1 tablespoon rapeseed oil, plus
    1 teaspoon
300g purple aubergine, sliced
    into 1cm x 3cm strips
1 red chilli, deseeded and finely
    sliced
1 tablespoon Shaohsing rice
    wine or dry sherry

For the sauce

1 teaspoon smooth peanut butter
1 tablespoon chilli bean paste
1 teaspoon sesame paste, such
    as tahini
2 tablespoons low-sodium light
    soy sauce
1 tablespoon Chinkiang black
    rice vinegar or balsamic
    vinegar
1 tablespoon cornflour
50ml cold water

For the garnish and to serve

1 spring onion, finely sliced
1 teaspoon toasted sesame
    seeds

I love Sichuan-style Fish Fragrant Aubergines, which is a spicy, pungent and salty dish, but I always feel it's missing a nutty sesame flavour. The addition of peanut butter and tahini takes this dish to another level – the perfect comfort dish. Serve with wheat flour noodles or steamed jasmine rice.

Serves 2 kcal 192 carbs 18.2g protein 4g fat 11.8g

Whisk together all the ingredients for the sauce in a jug, then set aside.

Heat a wok over a high heat until smoking and add 1 tablespoon rapeseed oil. Add the aubergine strips and stir-fry for 4-5 minutes while adding small drops of water to soften the aubergine – about 100ml in total. As the water evaporates, keep adding more. Once softened, push the aubergines to one side of the wok and add 1 teaspoon rapeseed oil. Fry the sliced chilli for a few seconds, then season with the Shaohsing rice wine or dry sherry.

Give the sauce a stir, then add to the wok and cook gently, stirring and tossing all the ingredients together until the sauce is heated through and has coated the aubergines – about 2 minutes.

Garnish with the spring onion and toasted sesame seeds and serve immediately.

V Ve DF

Chilli Bean Tofu with Enoki Mushrooms and Pak Choy

1 tablespoon rapeseed oil
2 small shallots, finely chopped
350g fresh firm tofu, drained and
    cut into 2cm cubes
1 tablespoon Shaohsing rice
    wine or dry sherry
200g baby pak choy, halved
100g fresh enoki mushrooms,
    stalks trimmed

For the sauce
100ml cold vegetable stock
1 tablespoon chilli bean paste
1 tablespoon low-sodium light
    soy sauce
½ teaspoon dark soy sauce
pinch of soft light brown sugar
1 teaspoon cornflour

For the garnish and to serve
teaspoon chilli oil
handful of fresh coriander,
    roughly chopped

Stewed dishes are, in my opinion, perfect winter food and here the tofu carries the spicy notes of the chilli bean paste and the seasonings so well. The enoki provide a stringy, sweet, soft texture while the pak choy brings a fresh peppery note to the dish. Perfect served with steamed jasmine rice or rice noodles.

Serves 2 kcal 276 carbs 13g protein 20.1g fat 15.3g

Whisk together all the ingredients for the sauce in a bowl, then set aside.

Heat a wok over a high heat until it starts to smoke, then add half the rapeseed oil. Stir-fry the shallots for 1 minute, then add the tofu cubes. Let the tofu sear and brown for 10 seconds on one side, then flip over. Add the Shaohsing rice wine or dry sherry and the pak choy leaves and toss together gently for 2 minutes to wilt the leaves.

Give the sauce a stir, then pour into the wok and bring to the boil. Add the enoki mushrooms and stir in to wilt.

Transfer to a serving plate, garnish with the chilli oil and chopped coriander and serve.

10 mins*

6-7 mins

* includes soaking the rice noodles

V DF

Vegetarian Char Kway Teow

1 tablespoon rapeseed oil

2 garlic cloves, finely chopped

2 small shallots, sliced

1 red cayenne chilli, deseeded and finely chopped

150g fried tofu, sliced into 1cm x 2.5cm strips

1/2 teaspoon medium curry powder

1 tablespoon Shaohsing rice wine

400g Thai or wide rice noodles, soaked in warm water for 5 minutes, then drained

pinch of caster sugar

2 tablespoons low-sodium light soy sauce

2 medium organic eggs, lightly beaten

80g fresh beansprouts

2 spring onions, sliced on the diagonal into 2.5cm pieces

For the garnish

1 red chilli, finely chopped, dressed in 1 tablespoon low-sodium light soy sauce

20g fried garlic and shallots (see page 22)

Char Kway Teow is one of my favourite wok-fried noodle dishes and the very best I have tried have been in Malaysia in Penang and Ipoh at the many street hawker stalls. This is my version; it comes originally from Chaozhou in China and there are many different versions. I like mine with fried tofu but you can use prawns or slices of pork too.

The trick is to use a small hint of medium curry powder for a warming spice note, and while Shaohsing rice wine is not a traditional ingredient it imparts a delicious sweetness. You can buy ready-to-eat wide rice noodles from most supermarkets, so this should be simple to prepare.

Serves 2 kcal 649 carbs 70.5g protein 31.3g fat 27.7g

Heat a wok over a high heat until smoking and add the rapeseed oil. Add the garlic, shallots and chilli and stir-fry for a few seconds to release the flavours. Add the fried tofu and curry powder and toss until all the tofu has turned crispy and golden yellow. Season with the Shaohsing rice wine or dry sherry, then add the noodles and toss for 2 minutes. Add the caster sugar and light soy sauce and ensure all the ingredients are covered in the seasoning.

Make a well in the centre of the mixture and pour in the beaten eggs. Leave to settle for a few seconds, then cook for half a minute, stirring and mixing the egg to combine with the noodles. Add the beansprouts and spring onions and toss together for 30 seconds until the beansprouts have wilted slightly.

Transfer to a serving plate. Garnish with the finely chopped chilli and sprinkle with the crispy fried garlic shallots. Serve immediately.

20 mins*

8 mins

* includes soaking time for the mushrooms and noodles

V Ve DF

1 tablespoon rapeseed oil
knob of fresh root ginger, peeled and cut into thick coin slices
2 small shallots, finely sliced
1 medium red chilli, deseeded and finely chopped
6 dried Chinese mushrooms, soaked in warm water for 20 minutes, then drained and sliced, stalks intact
½ teaspoon dark soy sauce
1 tablespoon Shaohsing rice wine or dry sherry
½ head Chinese leaf, sliced lengthways into thirds
1 litre hot vegetable stock
100g cauliflower florets, washed
350g fresh firm tofu, sliced into 1.5cm cubes
100g dried mung bean noodles, rehydrated in hot water for 5 minutes, then drained
1–2 tablespoons low-sodium light soy sauce
1 tablespoon Chinkiang black rice vinegar or balsamic vinegar
pinch of ground white pepper
pinch of sea salt flakes
small handful of fresh spinach leaves

For the garnish
1 teaspoon chilli oil
handful of fresh coriander leaves

Quick Cauliflower, Cabbage, Tofu and Spinach Casserole with Glass Noodles

Casseroles imply a lengthy cooking time but I promise this dish won't take hours. The cauliflower and Chinese leaves quickly soften to impart a delicate sweetness, the tofu absorbs all the umami richness in the broth and the mung bean noodles provide a slippery bite. It's moreish and yet light and delicious and so perfect for those in-between hot and cold days when you want something nutritious.

Serves 4 kcal 249 carbs 31.8g protein 11.7g fat 8.8g

Heat a wok over a high heat until smoking and add the rapeseed oil. Add the ginger, shallots, chilli and mushrooms and toss for 30 seconds to release their flavours. Season with the dark soy sauce and toss for a few more seconds, then add the Shaohsing rice wine or dry sherry.

Add the Chinese leaf, then pour in the hot vegetable stock. Add the cauliflower, tofu pieces and mung bean noodles and season with the light soy sauce to taste. Bring to the boil and cook for 4 minutes. Season with the vinegar, ground white pepper and salt to taste, then stir in the spinach and leave to wilt.

Transfer to large noodle bowls, garnish with the chilli oil and fresh coriander and serve immediately.

V Ve DF

Fish Fragrant Okra

1 tablespoon rapeseed oil

2 garlic cloves, crushed and
finely chopped

2.5cm piece of fresh root ginger,
peeled and grated

1 medium red chilli, deseeded
and finely chopped

1 tablespoon chilli bean sauce

300g okra, cut into 1cm slices

1 tablespoon Shaohsing rice
wine or dry sherry

1 spring onion, finely sliced,
to garnish

For the sauce

100ml cold vegetable stock

1 tablespoon low-sodium light
soy sauce

1 tablespoon Chinkiang black
rice vinegar or balsamic
vinegar

1 tablespoon cornflour

**This is an adaptation of Fish Fragrant Aubergines, a classic
Sichuan dish that is salty and spicy and perfect with rice.
Instead of using the Western aubergine or the long purple
Asian aubergine, I've decided to try it with okra. In my opinion,
the results are superb.**

Serves 2 kcal 165 carbs 20g protein 5.5g fat 7.5g

Whisk together all the ingredients for the sauce in a bowl, then
set aside.

Heat a wok over a high heat until smoking and add the rapeseed
oil. Add the garlic, ginger, chilli and chilli bean sauce and cook
for a few seconds. Add the okra and Shaohsing rice wine or dry
sherry, then pour the sauce over and bring to a quick boil. Cook,
stirring, until the sauce has thickened, then add in the spring
onion and serve immediately.

V Ve DF

Miso Asparagus with Shimeji

1 tablespoon rapeseed oil

1 garlic clove, peeled and finely
    chopped

1 medium red chilli, deseeded
    and finely chopped

12 tender baby asparagus stalks,
    cut on the angle into
    2.5cm slices

100g white shimeji mushrooms,
    individual stems separated

100g brown shimeji mushrooms,
    individual stems separated

For the sauce

50ml hot water

1 teaspoon red miso paste

1 tablespoon low-sodium light
    soy sauce

¼ teaspoon soft brown sugar

I love simple dishes like this one. Miso is a fermented soybean paste that contains good enzymes and bacteria and if you can find an organic red miso from a Japanese grocer the results will be superb. The miso imparts a rich savoury note to the stir-fry and, when mixed with sugar, gives a beany salty sweetness to the vegetables. Perfect served with brown rice and Japanese pickles.

Serves 2 kcal 94 carbs 4.5g protein 4.6g fat 6.4g

Whisk together all the ingredients for the sauce in a jug or bowl, then set aside.

Heat a wok over a high heat and, as the wok starts to smoke, add the rapeseed oil. Add the garlic and chilli and stir-fry for a few seconds to release their aroma, then add the baby asparagus and all the shimeji mushrooms. Toss together, then pour in the sauce and simmer for 1 minute, until the sauce has thickened and the vegetables are coated.

Transfer to a serving plate and serve immediately.

Tomato, Green Pepper, Chinese Cabbage and Spring Onion

1 tablespoon rapeseed oil

knob of fresh root ginger, peeled and grated

2 spring onions, finely sliced

4 ripe medium tomatoes, cored and sliced into quarters

1 green pepper, deseeded and finely chopped

½ Chinese cabbage, leaves separated and cut into 2.5cm slices

1 tablespoon Shaohsing rice wine or dry sherry

50ml cold vegetable stock

1 tablespoon low-sodium light soy sauce

1 teaspoon clear rice vinegar or cider vinegar

1 teaspoon cornflour blended with 1 tablespoon cold water

My grandmother used to make this simple vegetable stir-fry, which contains all the sour, peppery, sweet, pungent and umami notes that form the basis of Chinese cooking and make it so satisfying. For an additional spicy kick, serve with a side of your favourite chilli sauce or chilli oil and enjoy.

Serves 2 kcal 125 carbs 14.1g protein 3.4g fat 6.4g

Heat a wok over a high heat until smoking and add the rapeseed oil. Add the ginger and spring onions and stir-fry for a few seconds to release their flavours. Add the tomatoes, green pepper and Chinese cabbage and toss for 3 minutes, until the cabbage starts to wilt and the green pepper is tender.

Season with the Shaohsing rice wine or dry sherry and the vegetable stock. Stir in the light soy sauce and vinegar, then stir in the blended cornflour and simmer for a minute or so to thicken the sauce.

Transfer to a serving plate and serve immediately.

5 mins

8 mins

V DF

Bamboo Shoot Lo Mein

250g nest of thin egg noodles
    (400g cooked)
1 teaspoon toasted sesame oil,
    plus 1 tablespoon
1 tablespoon rapeseed oil
2 garlic cloves, finely chopped
1 tablespoon freshly grated
    root ginger
6 large fresh shiitake mushrooms,
    sliced, stems discarded
1 x 225g can of bamboo shoots,
    drained
200g choi sum, leaves and
    stalks cut into 5cm pieces,
    or broccoli florets
1 tablespoon Shaohsing rice
    wine or dry sherry
1 teaspoon dark soy sauce
large pinch of ground white
    pepper

For the Lo Mein sauce
300ml cold vegetable stock
150ml cold water
2 tablespoons low-sodium light
    soy sauce
1 tablespoon cornflour

Lo Mein is a Cantonese dish meaning 'stirred noodle'. Traditionally, Lo Mein is a variation of wonton noodles where all the components including the noodles are served separately. Lo Mein in Mandarin is known as 'Ban Mein' – i.e. mixed sauce noodle, and not necessarily stir-fried together but just tossed together. Don't be fazed by what seems like a long list of ingredients – precook the noodles, combine the ingredients for the sauce, stir-fry the main ingredients and toss the noodles and ingredients together in the sauce. You can also use whichever type of noodles you prefer, but thin or medium egg noodles work well.

Serves 2 kcal 529 carbs 73.2g protein 14.4g fat 20.5g

Whisk together all the ingredients for the Lo Mein sauce in a jug, then set aside.

Bring a pot of water to the boil, add the egg noodles and cook for 3 minutes until al dente. Drain under cold running water, then add 1 teaspoon toasted sesame oil to prevent the noodles from sticking together.

Heat a wok over a high heat until smoking and add the rapeseed oil. Add the garlic, ginger and shiitake mushrooms and toss together for a few seconds, then add the bamboo shoots and stir-fry for just under 1 minute. Add the choi sum and toss together for 1 minute, then pour in the Shaohsing rice wine or dry sherry and the Lo Mein sauce and bring to the boil, simmering for 1–2 minutes. Quickly add the cooked egg noodles and season with the dark soy sauce and 1 tablespoon toasted sesame oil. Stir together well for 1 minute, ensuring all the noodles are coated in the sauce. Season with the ground white pepper.

Transfer to a serving bowl and serve immediately.

CHING'S TIP
If using dried shiitake mushrooms instead of fresh, you can use the water the mushrooms were soaked in instead of the vegetable stock in the sauce.

10 mins
+ 5 mins

7 mins

V Ve DF

Red Cooked Shiitake Mushrooms, Pumpkin and Chestnuts

400g pumpkin flesh, sliced into 1.5cm cubes
pinch of salt flakes
1 tablespoon rapeseed oil
1 tablespoon whole five-spice with cinnamon bark (the cinnamon bark should be included in the spice mix when bought but, if not, you can add 1 piece)
10 fresh shiitake mushrooms, sliced
1 tablespoon Shaohsing rice wine or dry sherry
1 tablespoon low-sodium light soy sauce
1 teaspoon dark soy sauce
1 tablespoon brown sugar
10 cooked chestnuts
handful of fresh coriander leaves, to garnish

Whenever winter draws near, I find myself craving stews and braised dishes and automatically think of spiced chestnuts, pumpkins and earthy shiitake mushrooms. I love the Chinese red cooking technique, where dishes are stewed in a soy spiced liquid that imparts a warm red colour to the prepared food. It will keep your stomach happy through all the cold months.

Serves 2 kcal 224 carbs 35.4g protein 4.9g fat 8.2g

Heat a wok and add 1 litre cold water, then bring to the boil and add the pumpkin pieces. Season with salt and simmer for 8 minutes, until the pumpkin is cooked but still has a bite and retains its cube shape. Spoon out of the wok, drain and set aside.

Drain the wok and place over a high heat until smoking, then add the rapeseed oil. Swirl the oil around, then add the whole spices and stir-fry for a few seconds. Add the shiitake mushrooms and cook for 30 seconds until fragrant, then add the cooked pumpkin and the Shaohsing rice wine or dry sherry and cook for a further minute.

Add the light and dark soy sauces, pour in 150ml cold water, followed by the brown sugar and cooked chestnuts and bring it all to the boil, gently spooning the liquid over the ingredients. Cook until all the liquid has reduced by half and the ingredients are slightly sticky with the red glaze.

Take off the heat, garnish with some fresh coriander and serve immediately.

V Ve DF

Vegetarian Thai Aubergine Tom Yum Rice Noodle Soup

1 tablespoon rapeseed oil

1 teaspoon finely grated galangal or root ginger

1 stalk of lemongrass, finely sliced

1 whole kaffir lime leaf, fresh or dried

1 red chilli, deseeded and finely chopped

6 small green baby Thai aubergines, sliced into quarters

1 tablespoon vegetable bouillon powder

300g cooked flat wide rice noodles (150g dried), drizzled with sesame oil

150g fresh, firm tofu, drained and cut into 2cm cubes

4 cherry tomatoes

2 small heads of baby pak choy, halved

100ml reduced fat coconut milk

pinch of soft light brown sugar

1 tablespoon tamari or low-sodium light soy sauce

For the garnish

juice of 1 lime

small handful of Thai basil leaves, sliced into thin ribbons

small handful of fresh coriander, roughly chopped

Inspired by the flavours of Thai Hot and Sour Tom Yum Soup, I have made my own version. For Thais, wok-frying all the aromatics is not the correct way to start this recipe, but I love to use the wok to explode the spices in hot oil as I think it injects a slight smoky flavour and enriches the broth. If you can't find Thai aubergines, you can use 200g oyster mushrooms. You could turn this into a meat or seafood dish and use fish sauce for a salty edge, or adapt it for vegan friends by adding assorted greens. Versatile and delicious.

Serves 2 kcal 525 carbs 70g protein 17.9g fat 19.8g

Heat a wok over a high heat until smoking and add the rapeseed oil. Add the galangal or ginger, the lemongrass, kaffir lime leaf and red chilli and explode the flavours in the hot oil for 10 seconds. Add the aubergines and toss for 2 minutes (if using oyster mushrooms, cook for 1 minute).

Pour in 800ml cold water and season with the vegetable bouillon powder, then cook for 10 minutes on a high heat to infuse all the flavours. Once it has come to the boil, add the rice noodles, tofu, cherry tomatoes and pak choy. Season with the coconut milk, soft brown sugar and tamari or soy sauce, then bring back to the boil and simmer for a minute.

Transfer to serving bowls and garnish with the lime juice, Thai basil and fresh coriander.

15 mins

10 mins

V DF

Veggie Dan Dan Mein

200g dried wheat flour noodles

pinch of sea salt flakes

1 teaspoon toasted sesame oil

500ml hot vegetable stock

1 tablespoon peanut oil

2 garlic cloves, finely chopped

1 tablespoon grated root ginger

3 red chillies, deseeded and
    finely chopped

300g Quorn mince

100g cornichons (or Chinese
    Zha Cai), finely chopped

1 tablespoon Shaohsing rice
    wine or dry sherry

1 tablespoon Chinkiang black rice
    vinegar or balsamic vinegar

1 tablespoon low-sodium light
    soy sauce

1 teaspoon Chinese sesame
    paste

½ teaspoon ground dry-toasted
    Sichuan peppercorns

freshly ground white pepper

For the chilli oil dressing

1 tablespoon chilli oil

1 tablespoon toasted sesame oil

1 tablespoon low-sodium light
    soy sauce

pinch of ground dry-toasted
    Sichuan peppercorns

1 red chilli, deseeded and diced

For the garnish

1 large spring onion, finely sliced
    on the diagonal

fresh coriander leaves, chopped

I love using Quorn mince for this Sichuan dish as it makes it moreish but also light. The peppercorns then give it a lovely numbing zinginess, which I find rather addictive!

Serves 2 kcal 678 carbs 85.7g protein 37.2g fat 18.2g

Whisk together all the ingredients for the chilli oil dressing in a small bowl and set aside.

Bring a large pot of water to the boil over a high heat and add the dried noodles. Season with salt, then stir and cook until al dente – about 4 minutes. Drain, rinse with cold water, then shake out any excess liquid and transfer the noodles to a bowl. Drizzle over the toasted sesame oil, toss to coat well and set aside.

Place the vegetable stock in a saucepan and bring to a gentle simmer. Heat a wok over a high heat until smoking and add the peanut oil. Add the garlic, ginger and chillies and stir-fry for 30 seconds, then add the Quorn mince and cook for 2–3 minutes until browned. Add the cornichons, the Shaohsing rice wine or dry sherry, the vinegar, soy sauce, sesame paste and ground peppercorns and stir well until the Quorn mince takes on the flavourings. Season with ground white pepper and remove from the heat.

To serve, divide the noodles and Quorn mince between two large soup bowls, and ladle hot stock on top. Garnish with the spring onion and coriander and serve with a spoonful of the chilli oil dressing to taste. Serve immediately.

CHING'S TIP
Sesame paste can be substituted with an equal amount of tahini mixed with 1 teaspoon toasted sesame oil.

10 mins

5 mins

V Ve DF

Spicy Coriander Chickpea Fried Rice

1 tablespoon rapeseed oil

2 garlic cloves, crushed and finely chopped

1 small red onion, diced

1 red pepper, deseeded and diced

1 green pepper, deseeded and diced

400g can of chickpeas, drained

200g cooked jasmine and wild rice mix

1 tablespoon red wine vinegar

1 tablespoon low-sodium light soy sauce

pinch of dried chilli flakes

pinch of sea salt flakes

pinch of ground black pepper

juice of 1 lime

3 tablespoons finely chopped fresh coriander

This is a store cupboard fried rice that is perfect for a quick mid-week veggie supper. Chickpeas are a high source of protein and I think taste great in this dish together with the tangy vinegar and crunchy peppers.

Serves 2 kcal 355 carbs 55.6g protein 13.8g fat 10.2g

Heat a wok until smoking and add the rapeseed oil. Stir-fry the garlic and red onion for 1 minute, then add the red and green peppers and toss for 30 seconds. Add the chickpeas and rice and toss for 1 minute.

Season with the red wine vinegar, light soy sauce, dried chilli flakes, salt and ground black pepper and cook, stirring, for 30 seconds. Sprinkle with the lime juice, then stir in the finely chopped coriander and serve immediately.

20
mins*

5
mins

*** includes soaking time
for the mushrooms and
noodles**

V Ve DF

Japchae – Korean Stir-fried Mixed Vegetable Noodles

150g uncooked sweet potato
thread noodles
1 tablespoon rapeseed oil
1 garlic clove, crushed and finely
chopped
½ medium white onion, sliced
3 dried Chinese mushrooms,
soaked in hot water for
20 minutes, drained, stalks
discarded, cut into 1cm slices
1 tablespoon Shaohsing rice
wine or dry sherry
1 medium carrot, sliced into
matchsticks
120g Chinese leaf, shredded
2 spring onions, cut into
2.5cm slices
100g baby spinach leaves
1 teaspoon toasted sesame
seeds, to garnish

For the sauce
1 tablespoon toasted sesame oil
2 tablespoons low-sodium light
soy sauce
1 tablespoon Shaohsing rice
wine or dry sherry
1 teaspoon Korean gochujang
chilli paste
½ teaspoon caster sugar
pinch of ground white pepper

There are many versions of this delicious noodle dish the world over but this one is very easy to make at home. I like to use traditional sweet potato starch noodles, which you can buy from a Korean supermarket or online, as they have a great texture and the *gochujang* (Korean chilli bean paste), which gives them a delicious smoky spiciness, is my personal addition.

Serves 2 kcal 444 carbs 71.5g protein 9g fat 13.7g

Whisk together all the ingredients for the sauce in a jug, then set aside.

Cook the noodles in boiling water for 10 minutes, then drain, rinse in cold water and cut into 12.5cm lengths.

Heat a wok over a high heat until smoking and add the rapeseed oil. Add the garlic and stir-fry for a few seconds, then add the onion and cook for 10 seconds. Add the mushrooms and toss for 5 seconds, then add the Shaohsing rice wine or dry sherry and swirl around the pan. Add the carrot, Chinese cabbage and spring onions and toss for 30 seconds. Drizzle in the water around the edge of the wok to create steam to help cook the vegetables. Add the spinach and noodles and toss to heat through, then stir in the sauce and cook for 10 seconds.

Remove from the heat and transfer to a serving plate. Garnish with the sesame seeds and serve immediately.

10 mins

8 mins

V DF

Spicy Potato and Egg Stir-fry

350g potatoes, peeled

pinch of sea salt flakes

3 medium organic eggs

1 teaspoon toasted sesame oil

pinch of ground white pepper

2 tablespoons rapeseed oil

2 tablespoons finely chopped garlic

knob of fresh root ginger, peeled and grated

1 red chilli, deseeded and finely chopped

1 spring onion, finely sliced

2 tablespoons pickled chillies in vinegar

1 teaspoon ground dry-toasted Sichuan peppercorns

2 tablespoons Shaohsing rice wine or dry sherry

pinch of caster sugar

2 tablespoons chilli oil

For the garnish

10g toasted white sesame seeds

small handful of fresh coriander, chopped

The wonderful cook Ms Xingyun Chen, aunt of our friend Jenny Gao, made me a deliciously spicy and crisp potato stir-fry whilst I was filming *Exploring China* with Ken Hom, for the BBC and I've recreated it many times since. I also like to add a little beaten egg that, if you are vegan, you can leave out.

Serves 2 kcal 523 carbs 38.3g protein 16.7g fat 34.8g

Cut the potatoes into thin slices, then stack them up and slice into matchstick-size pieces. Soak them in a bowl of cold water with a pinch of salt for 5 minutes. Drain and blot dry with paper towels, then set aside.

Crack the eggs into a bowl, season with the toasted sesame oil, salt and ground white pepper and beat lightly to combine.

Heat a wok over a high heat until smoking and add the rapeseed oil. Add the garlic, ginger, chilli, spring onion, pickled chillies and ground Sichuan peppercorns, then stir-fry for 10 seconds to release their flavours. Add the potato matchsticks and toss for 1 minute until they are coated with all the ingredients. Season with the Shaohsing rice wine or dry sherry and the sugar and toss well to combine.

Make a well in the centre of the wok, pour in the beaten egg mixture and cook, stirring, until the eggs are lightly scrambled and still moist. Toss together, season with chilli oil and add more salt if necessary. Transfer to a serving plate, garnish with sesame seeds and freshly chopped coriander and serve immediately.

10 mins

20 mins*

* includes cooking the rice

V GF DF

Asparagus, Carrot, Shiitake and Egg White Congee

1 tablespoon rapeseed oil

knob of fresh root ginger, peeled and grated

2 medium carrots, finely diced into 5mm cubes

¼ teaspoon ground turmeric

½ teaspoon fennel seeds

200g tender asparagus spears, cut into 2.5cm pieces

small handful of fresh shiitake mushrooms, sliced

300g cooked jasmine rice (150g uncooked)

1 tablespoon Shaohsing rice wine or dry sherry

550ml hot vegetable stock

1–2 tablespoons tamari

1 teaspoon toasted sesame oil

pinch of ground white pepper

3 large organic egg whites, lightly beaten (save the egg yolks for an omelette)

1 spring onion, finely sliced, to garnish

This bowl of congee delivers the perfect nourishing comfort food. The ginger, fennel and turmeric spice up the vegetables and warm the whole body and offer the promise of an instant lift on a glum day. Vegans can omit the egg and throw in strips of smoked tofu.

Serves 2 kcal 342 carbs 50.2g protein 15.7g fat 10.5g

Heat a wok over a high heat until smoking and add the rapeseed oil. Add the ginger and carrots and stir-fry for 1 minute. Season with the turmeric and fennel seeds, then add the asparagus and mushrooms and continue to cook on a high heat to sear the vegetables.

Tip in the cooked jasmine rice and stir-fry for 1 minute. Add the Shaohsing rice wine or dry sherry, followed by the hot vegetable stock and bring to the boil, then season to taste with tamari, sesame oil and ground white pepper.

Stir in the beaten egg whites and swirl them in the soupy rice to cook. Ladle out into bowls and sprinkle with the spring onion.

12 mins

5 mins

V DF

Chinese Wok-fried Spicy Spring Onion Salsa Verde with Kale and Egg Noodles

120g curly kale, sliced
200g dried egg noodles
1 teaspoon toasted sesame oil
2 tablespoons rapeseed oil
pinch of sea salt flakes
knob of fresh root ginger, peeled
    and grated
1 red chilli, deseeded and finely
    sliced at an angle
pinch of dried chilli flakes
2 spring onions, finely chopped
50ml cold vegetable stock
1 tablespoon low-sodium light
    soy sauce

In Chinese cuisine there is a ginger and spring onion sauce that is often dressed over steamed chicken, which I adore. I also love to use this sauce for a veggie chow mein – it's simple and just divine.

Serves 2 kcal 482 carbs 75.6g protein 14.9g fat 15.7g

Pour 1 litre cold water into a pan and bring to the boil. Add the kale and blanch for 30 seconds, then drain and set aside. Cook the noodles according to the packet instructions, then run them under the cold tap, drain and drizzle with the toasted sesame oil.

Heat a wok over a high heat until smoking and add the rapeseed oil. Add the salt and let it dissolve in the hot oil, then add the ginger, fresh chilli, dried chilli and spring onions in quick succession to explode their flavours in the wok.

Add the vegetable stock and stir-fry on a medium heat for 30 seconds. Add the kale and cooked egg noodles and toss all the ingredients together to warm through. Season with the light soy sauce and give it one final toss, then transfer to serving plates and eat immediately.

Taiwanese Veggie Dan Zai Noodles

300g cooked egg noodles
(150g dried)
1 teaspoon toasted sesame oil
1 tablespoon rapeseed oil
1 small garlic clove, grated
2 small shallots, finely chopped
160g Quorn mince
1 teaspoon dark soy sauce
50g Chinese leaf, leaves and
stalks separated, cut into
1cm slices
1 tablespoon Shaohsing rice
wine or dry sherry
50ml vegetable stock
2 tablespoons low-sodium
light soy sauce
1 teaspoon toasted sesame oil

For the garnish
25g Chinese chive flowers
chopped into 4cm pieces
(or spring onion cut into
2.5cm pieces)
handful of beansprouts
1 teaspoon toasted sesame oil
1 small garlic clove, minced

This is based on a famous street market dish in Taiwan called Dan Zai Mein. Traditionally, pork mince and shrimp head juices are used to create a delicious stock for a soup-like dish. My version is vegetarian and uses just the cooking juices from the wok, but it's equally moreish and delicious.

Serves 2 kcal 464 carbs 52.5g protein 22.1g fat 17.8g

If using dried egg noodles, cook the noodles in boiling water for 3 minutes, then drain and refresh in cold water. Drizzle the noodles with the toasted sesame oil and put to one side.

Heat a wok over a high heat until smoking and add the rapeseed oil, then stir-fry the garlic and shallots for just under 1 minute. Add the minced Quorn and toss for 1 minute until brown and caramelised, then season with the dark soy sauce, add the cabbage leaves and stalks and stir-fry for 1 minute. Add the Shaohsing rice wine or dry sherry and cook until evaporated. Add the vegetable stock and cook for 2 minutes until the cabbage has wilted, then season with the light soy sauce. Stir-fry all the ingredients until brown and slightly caramelised, then season with the toasted sesame oil and turn the heat right down to keep warm.

Pour 1 litre cold water into a medium pan, bring to the boil and blanch the Chinese chive flowers and beansprouts for 10 seconds, then remove and drain. Drizzle with the toasted sesame oil to prevent them from sticking together.

Ladle a little Quorn and cabbage mixture into a large serving bowl. Place some noodles on top and spoon over more of the mixture. Place the chives and beansprouts on the side, then garnish with the minced garlic. Serve immediately.

Egg, Asparagus, Corn and Shiitake Mushroom Fried Rice

3 large eggs, lightly beaten
pinch of sea salt flakes
pinch of ground white pepper,
    plus ¼ teaspoon
2 tablespoons rapeseed oil
2 garlic cloves, finely chopped
125g baby asparagus spears,
    sliced into 1cm rounds, tips cut
    into 2cm slices
kernels from 1 fresh sweetcorn
80g fresh shiitake mushrooms,
    stems separated, thinly sliced
400g cooked cold jasmine rice
    (200g uncooked)
2 tablespoons low-sodium light
    soy sauce
1 teaspoon toasted sesame oil
1 red chilli, deseeded and finely
    chopped, to garnish

I love fried rice – the perfect balance between comfort food and healthy food – and especially this combination of asparagus rounds and fresh shiitake mushrooms. I've worked with revered wok masters in Hong Kong who scramble the egg first to get fluffy pieces of egg within the rice dish and so I've used this technique here. This flavourful light dish will make the perfect accompaniment to many of your favourite Chinese dishes or it would be perfect as a meal on its own with a good side of chilli sauce.

Serves 2 kcal 529 carbs 68.2g protein 19.2g fat 21.8g

Lightly beat the eggs in a bowl and season with sea salt and ground white pepper.

Heat a wok over a medium heat and add 1 tablespoon rapeseed oil. Pour in the beaten eggs and stir to lightly scramble. When the egg has turned golden and is still fluffy, take off the heat, transfer the eggs to a bowl and set aside.

To cook the rice, reheat the wok over a high heat and, when it starts to smoke, add 1 tablespoon rapeseed oil. Add the garlic and stir quickly for a few seconds, then add the asparagus and sweetcorn and cook for 2 minutes until the asparagus starts to turn a deeper green and the sweetcorn a golden yellow. Add the mushrooms and toss together, then add the cooked rice. Stir well and toss to combine all the ingredients, then cook for 1–2 minutes. Season with the light soy sauce and stir again.

Return the scrambled eggs to the wok, season with the toasted sesame oil and remaining ground white pepper and give it a few more stirs.

Transfer to a large serving plate and garnish with the chopped chilli. Serve immediately.

10 mins*

5 mins

V DF

Leek, Shiitake and Beansprouts on Thin Egg Noodles

1 tablespoon rapeseed oil

100g baby leeks, sliced on the angle into 2.5cm pieces

100g dried Chinese mushrooms, soaked in warm water for 20 minutes, drained and stalks discarded, cut into 1cm slices

½ teaspoon dark soy sauce

1 tablespoon Shaohsing rice wine or dry sherry

300g cooked thin egg noodles (150g dried), drained and dressed with 1 teaspoon toasted sesame oil

1 tablespoon mushroom sauce or oyster sauce

pinch of caster sugar

2 tablespoons low-sodium light soy sauce

handful of beansprouts

1 teaspoon toasted sesame oil

1 spring onion, finely sliced

This is a simple yet rich-tasting dish. The trick is to find plump dried Chinese mushrooms, which can be bought from a Chinese supermarket, as their earthy umami, meaty flavour contrasts beautifully with the texture of the egg noodles. Delicious!

Serves 2 kcal 511 carbs 79.7g protein 15.3g fat 15.6g

Heat a wok over a high heat until smoking and add the rapeseed oil. Add the baby leeks and toss for 30 seconds, then add the rehydrated mushrooms and toss for 10 seconds to release their flavours. Add the dark soy sauce and toss well, then add the Shaohsing rice wine or dry sherry and cook until evaporated.

Add the noodles and toss together well for 30 seconds, then season with the mushroom or oyster sauce, sugar and light soy sauce. Add the beansprouts and gently toss and fold into the dish.

Season with the toasted sesame oil, garnish with the spring onion and serve immediately.

Egg Foo Yung

1 tablespoon rapeseed oil
1 garlic clove, finely chopped
small handful of fresh shiitake
    mushrooms, cut into 1cm
    slices, stalks discarded
1 tablespoon Shaohsing rice
    wine or dry sherry
2 large cos leaves, cut into
    2.5cm slices

For the sauce
120ml cold vegetable stock
¼ teaspoon dark soy sauce
1 tablespoon low-sodium light
    soy sauce
1 tablespoon cornflour
1 teaspoon toasted sesame oil

For the omelette
1 tablespoon rapeseed oil
1 garlic clove, finely chopped
small handful of beansprouts
1 medium carrot, grated
5 eggs, lightly beaten, seasoned
    with a pinch each of sea
    salt flakes and ground white
    pepper and a dash of toasted
    sesame oil
1 spring onion, finely sliced on
    the diagonal into horse ear
    shapes

A humble Chinese omelette made using leftovers, and served with soy gravy and rice, Egg Foo Yung is thought to have been invented by Chinese immigrants who came to America during the nineteenth century Gold Rush. This is my version. I like to add garlic and fresh shiitake mushrooms to create a rich umami gravy, then carrot, beansprouts and spring onions, and serve it with a hit of crunchy sliced cos lettuce leaves. It makes a great light supper with or without rice.

Serves 2 kcal 393 carbs 15.3g protein 21.2g fat 27.7g

Whisk together all the ingredients for the sauce in a bowl, then set aside.

Heat a wok over a high heat until smoking and add 1 teaspoon rapeseed oil. Add the garlic and stir-fry for a few seconds, then add the shiitake mushrooms. Toss for a few seconds, then add the Shaohsing rice wine or dry sherry.

Pour in the sauce and bring to a simmer, stirring, until the sauce has thickened and is glossy and shiny. Transfer the mushroom gravy to a glass heatproof jug, cover with foil and keep warm.

Give the wok a quick rinse with water then place over a high heat to make the omelette. Add 1 tablespoon rapeseed oil, then add the garlic and stir-fry for a few seconds. Add the beansprouts and carrot and toss for 1 minute, then pour in the seasoned beaten eggs and leave to settle for a few seconds. Slowly unfurl the sides of the omelette, loosening them with a flat spatula, and cook for a further 20 seconds. Sprinkle with the spring onion, then flip it over and cook for a few more seconds.

Transfer the omelette to a serving plate, pour the mushroom gravy over the top and garnish with the cos lettuce leaves in the centre for a crunchy freshness.

Chinese Black Bean and Courgette Scramble

1 tablespoon rapeseed oil
1 garlic clove, finely chopped
1 red chilli, deseeded and finely
   chopped
2 medium courgettes, cut into
   1cm slices
1 teaspoon fermented salted
   black beans, rinsed, crushed
   and mixed with 1 tablespoon
   Shaohsing rice wine or
   dry sherry
1 tablespoon low-sodium light
   soy sauce
4 eggs, lightly beaten, seasoned
   with a pinch of salt and
   1 teaspoon toasted sesame oil

For the garnish
drizzle of sriracha chilli sauce
5g fresh coriander leaves

This is a tribute to my grandmother's farm-style cooking. She would fuse traditional southern Chinese ingredients, such as fermented salted black beans, with vegetables or eggs to create a delicious meal. Fermented salted black beans can be bought from a Chinese grocer online – they are the next best things to salt! This would make a great breakfast or brunch – add some creamy avocado slices on top of the scramble if you like. I think grandmother would love this dish.

Serves 2 kcal 270 carbs 6.4g protein 19.6g fat 18.5g

Heat a wok over a high heat until smoking and add the rapeseed oil. Add the garlic and chilli and toss for 5 seconds to release their flavours, then add the courgettes and toss on a high heat for 1 minute. Add the fermented salted black bean mixture and toss for 2 minutes until the courgettes have softened but still have a crunchy texture, then season with the light soy sauce and toss together well.

Pour in the seasoned beaten eggs and stir to scramble, being careful not to break up the courgette pieces. Once the scrambled eggs are soft and golden, transfer to a serving plate.

Garnish with sriracha and coriander for an aromatic finish and serve immediately.

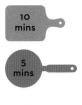

Beijing Egg and Tomato Noodle Soup

V DF

knob of fresh root ginger, peeled
and grated
250g medium-size tomatoes,
cored and quartered
100g Chinese leaves, cut into
2cm slices
5 fresh shiitake mushrooms,
rinsed, dried and cut into
1cm thick slices
1 tablespoon vegetable bouillon
powder
300g cooked wide flat rice
noodles (150g uncooked)
1 tablespoon low-sodium light
soy sauce
pinch of ground white pepper
1 tablespoon toasted sesame oil
1 egg, beaten
2 spring onions, sliced on the
diagonal into 1cm pieces,
to garnish

**Based on a snack recipe from Northern China, this egg and
tomato soup would be cooked with *la-mein* (hand-pulled
noodles) and served from small stalls for breakfast or as a light
supper. It was commonly referred to as 'Egg Flower Soup',
because the egg swirls created a flowery pattern. Traditional
wheat flour noodles or wide flat noodles are perfect for this
dish as they have a silky texture.**

Serves 2 kcal 409 carbs 63.3g protein 11.3g fat 13.1g

Pour 1 litre boiling water into a wok. Add the ginger, tomatoes,
Chinese leaves, shiitake mushrooms and vegetable stock
powder, then bring to the boil and cook for about 2 minutes to
soften the vegetables. Turn the heat down to medium and add
the rice noodles. Season with the light soy sauce, white pepper
and toasted sesame oil and stir in.

Take a fork or spoon and make a swirling, stirring motion in the
broth, then add the beaten egg and continue to swirl until the
egg is cooked (it will make a web-like pattern).

Ladle the soup into two large bowls, garnish with the spring
onions and eat immediately.

Fish &

shellfish

5 mins

30 secs

DF

Radish in Black Rice Vinegar with Crabmeat and Black Sesame Seeds

1 teaspoon rapeseed oil
300g radish leaves
200g radishes, cut into
    5mm slices
1 tablespoon Chinkiang black
    rice vinegar or balsamic
    vinegar
pinch of caster sugar
200g fresh white crabmeat
5g black sesame seeds,
    to garnish
pinch of dried chilli flakes,
    to garnish

Radishes taste really great when they've been lightly stir-fried as the cooking brings out their sweetness, which in turn perfectly complements the sweetness of the crabmeat. Sesame seeds balance this out with a little nuttiness and the chilli adds a subtle hint of spice.

Serves 2 kcal 213 carbs 9.1g protein 26.2g fat 8g

Heat a wok over a high heat until smoking and add the rapeseed oil. Add the radish leaves and sliced radish and toss for 10 seconds, then drizzle 30ml cold water in around the edge of the wok to create some steam to help cook the radish. Season immediately with the vinegar and sugar and toss through.

Spoon the radish onto serving plates, then top with the fresh crabmeat and garnish with the sesame seeds and chilli flakes.

25*
mins

5
mins

* includes cooking the rice

DF

1 tablespoon rapeseed oil, plus
1 teaspoon
2 garlic cloves, finely chopped
200g white cabbage leaves
(keep the centre stalk for
vegetable stock), leaves torn
into bite-size pieces
1 tablespoon Shaohsing rice
wine or dry sherry
3 tablespoons vegetable stock
350g cooked and cooled jasmine
rice (175g uncooked)
200g cooked tiger prawns
50g cooked frozen peas
1 tablespoon low-sodium light
soy sauce
1 tablespoon oyster sauce
large pinch of freshly ground
white pepper
1 teaspoon toasted sesame oil

Tiger Prawn and Cabbage Fried Rice

I love to add cabbage to fried rice, as it imparts a sweet crunchiness to the dish and, when paired with wok-fried garlic, it is some kind of wonderful! You can use cooked giant tiger prawns for quicker results, but ensure you choose a good-quality variety and move fast once they are added to the wok, as you don't want them to turn rubbery.

Serves 2 kcal 435 carbs 66.8g protein 23.7g fat 10g

Heat a wok over a high heat until smoking and add 1 tablespoon rapeseed oil. Add the garlic and stir-fry for a few seconds, then add the cabbage and stir-fry for 1 minute. Season with the Shaohsing rice wine or dry sherry, then add the vegetable stock to create steam to help cook the cabbage. Cook for another minute until the cabbage has softened. (If there is any excess liquid in the wok, pour it into a small bowl and reserve to use as a seasoning later if the rice is a little dry).

Return the wok to the heat, push the cabbage to one side and add 1 teaspoon rapeseed oil. Add the jasmine rice and fry together for 1 minute, then add the tiger prawns and peas and toss until all the ingredients are thoroughly combined.

Season with the light soy sauce, oyster sauce, ground white pepper and toasted sesame oil and toss together well. Serve immediately.

5 mins

4 mins

DF

Prawns with Shishito Peppers

2 tablespoons rapeseed oil

pinch of sea salt flakes

1 garlic clove, crushed and
finely chopped

1 red chilli, deseeded and
finely chopped

200g shishito peppers, left
whole

300g cooked giant Madagascan
prawns or raw tiger prawns

1 tablespoon mirin

2 tablespoons low-sodium
light soy sauce

juice of 1 lime

pinch of caster sugar

This is a delicious spicy dish – I love the heat of shishito peppers, especially not knowing whether the next hit will be sweet and peppery or sweet and POW! It is a bit of a roulette-type situation, so be careful if you are not into spicy food. You can always use green pepper strips as a substitute. Enjoy!

Serves 2 kcal 254 carbs 11g protein 26.1g fat 11.9g

Heat a wok over a high heat until smoking and add the rapeseed oil. Add the salt and let it dissolve in the hot oil. Add the garlic and red chilli and toss for a few seconds. Add the shishito peppers, toss for 30 seconds until they are seared on the outside and beginning to soften, then stir-fry for another minute. Add the cooked prawns and toss for less than 1 minute (or cook the raw prawns for 2–3 minutes, depending on their size). Season with the sake or mirin, the light soy sauce, lime juice and sugar and stir to combine.

Transfer to serving plates and serve immediately.

Oyster Sauce Scallops and Mangetout

1 tablespoon rapeseed oil
knob of fresh root ginger, peeled
  and grated
8 medium-sized scallops
1 tablespoon Shaohsing rice
  wine or dry sherry
100g mangetout, left whole
1 teaspoon oyster sauce
1 tablespoon low-sodium light
  soy sauce
1 teaspoon toasted sesame oil

The umami oyster sauce is a great partner for the sweet prawns and the mangetout deliver a lovely sweet crunch. Use the freshest scallops you can get hold of and you cannot go wrong.

Serves 2 kcal 133 carbs 5.1g protein 10.5g fat 7.5g

Heat a wok over a high heat until smoking and add the rapeseed oil. Add the ginger and toss for a few seconds to release its flavour. Add the scallops and cook for 5 seconds until seared and browned, then flip them over. Season with the Shaohsing rice wine or dry sherry, then add the mangetout and stir-fry for 5 seconds. Add a small splash of water around the edge of the wok to create some steam to help cook the mangetout, then season with the oyster sauce and light soy sauce and toss to coat well.

Drizzle in the toasted sesame oil, then transfer to a serving bowl and serve immediately.

5 mins

5 mins

DF

Spicy Honey Garlic Prawns with Water Chestnuts

1 tablespoon rapeseed oil

2 garlic cloves, crushed and finely chopped

knob of fresh root ginger, peeled and grated

1 red chilli, deseeded and finely chopped

200g raw tiger prawns, shelled and deveined

1 tablespoon Shaohsing rice wine or dry sherry

1 x 225g can of water chestnuts, drained

1 teaspoon chilli bean paste

1 tablespoon runny honey

1 tablespoon low-sodium light soy sauce

2 spring onions, cut on an angle into 1cm slices, to garnish

This is a quick and easy stir-fry dish, perfect for when you need dinner on the table in minutes. And if you use cooked tiger prawns it will be on the table in seconds! Well, maybe not seconds...but you get the idea.

Serves 2 kcal 193 carbs 15.2g protein 19.4g fat 6.4g

Heat a wok over a high heat until smoking and add the rapeseed oil. Add the garlic, ginger and chilli and stir-fry for a few seconds to release their aroma. Add the tiger prawns and leave to sear and brown for a few seconds, then flip them over and cook for 1 minute. Season with the Shaohsing rice wine or dry sherry.

Add the water chestnuts and toss well, then add the chilli bean paste, honey and light soy sauce and toss for a few seconds to mix the sauces well.

Garnish with the spring onions and serve immediately.

DF

Lobster Tails, Baby Asparagus and Eggs in Hot Bean Sauce

1 tablespoon rapeseed oil

2 garlic cloves, crushed and finely chopped

knob of fresh root ginger, peeled and grated

1 red chilli, deseeded and finely chopped

200g cooked fresh lobster or crayfish tails, sliced into 2.5cm cubes

1 tablespoon Shaohsing rice wine or dry sherry

100g baby asparagus spears, cut on the angle into 2.5cm slices

1 teaspoon yellow bean paste

1/2 teaspoon dark soy sauce

1 tablespoon low-sodium light soy sauce

100ml hot vegetable stock

1 egg, lightly beaten

1 teaspoon cornflour blended with 1 tablespoon cold water

2 spring onions, sliced into strips and soaked in iced water for 5 minutes to curl, to garnish

This is a decadent stir-fry using lobster tails and the freshest baby asparagus in season. Pungent and aromatic with a hint of chilli spice, it is perfect for dinner guests and fuss-free to make. You can also turn this into a saucy noodle dish – just up the quantities for the sauce and seasoning, add cooked thin egg noodles at the end and wok it all together.

Serves 2 kcal 238 carbs 7.8g protein 28.5g fat 10.4g

Heat a wok over a high heat until smoking and add the rapeseed oil. Add the garlic, ginger and chilli and stir-fry for a few seconds to release their flavours. Add the cooked lobster or crayfish and toss for 5 seconds. Season with the Shaohsing rice wine or dry sherry, then add the asparagus and toss for 10 seconds. Drizzle in a tablespoon of cold water around the edge of the wok to create steam to help cook the asparagus. Add the yellow bean paste, dark soy sauce and light soy sauce and toss for 10 seconds, then add the hot vegetable stock and bring to the boil.

Stir in the beaten egg and bring back to the boil. Add the blended cornflour and stir in to thicken the sauce and bring all the flavours together.

Garnish with the spring onion curls and serve immediately.

CHING'S TIP

Work quickly to avoid overcooking the lobster.

---

10 mins

5 mins

DF

Spicy Oyster Sauce Squid with Green Peppers

1 tablespoon rapeseed oil

1 medium white onion, halved and cut into slices

1 red chilli, deseeded and finely chopped

200g whole baby squid, sliced into rings

1 tablespoon Shaohsing rice wine or dry sherry

1 green pepper, deseeded and sliced into 1cm cubes

1 tablespoon low-sodium light soy sauce

1 teaspoon oyster sauce

1/2 teaspoon dark soy sauce

1 tablespoon fresh lemon juice

pinch of caster sugar

I love how the savoury-sour combination of the oyster sauce and rice vinegar complements the delicate flavour of the baby squid. However, be careful you don't overcook the squid as it can all too quickly turn to rubber. The trick is to sear it very quickly in a very hot pan. Don't take your eye off it.

Serves 2 kcal 182 carbs 11.8g protein 17.4g fat 7.6g

Heat a wok over a high heat until smoking and add the rapeseed oil. Add the onion and toss for 20 seconds until seared, softened and brown at the edges. Add the chilli and baby squid and toss for 10 seconds, then season with the Shaohsing rice wine or dry sherry.

Add the green pepper and toss for 1 minute. Drizzle a tablespoon of cold water in around the edge of the wok to create steam to help cook the pepper. Cook for another minute, then season with the light soy sauce, oyster sauce, dark soy sauce, lemon juice and sugar and serve immediately.

Hot and Sour Mackerel Fillets on Spinach and Cos

200g mackerel fillet, sliced into
    1cm thick strips
pinch of Chinese five-spice
    powder
pinch of sea salt flakes
pinch of ground black pepper
1 tablespoon cornflour
1 tablespoon rapeseed oil
2 garlic cloves, crushed and
    finely chopped
1 red chilli, deseeded and finely
    chopped
1 tablespoon Shaohsing rice
    wine or dry sherry

For the dressing
1 tablespoon low-sodium light
    soy sauce
1 tablespoon rice vinegar
pinch of dried chilli flakes
pinch of caster sugar
1 tablespoon toasted sesame oil
1 teaspoon chilli oil

To garnish and serve
100g cos lettuce leaves, sliced
    into 2.5cm pieces
150g spinach leaves
1 spring onion, finely sliced

To me, this dish is the perfect combination of hot and cold and light and fresh. I especially like how the crunchy cos and fresh spinach leaves contrast with the hot-sour dressing.

Serves 2 kcal 420 carbs 13.8g protein 21.7g fat 31.3g

Whisk together all the ingredients for the dressing in a jug, then set aside.

Put the mackerel strips in a small bowl and season with the five-spice powder, sea salt and ground black pepper, then dust with the cornflour.

Heat a wok over a high heat until smoking and add the rapeseed oil. Add the garlic and chilli and toss for a few seconds. Add the mackerel strips and leave to sear on one side for 5 seconds, then deglaze with 1 tablespoon of Shaohsing rice wine and using a spatula carefully lift and turn the fillets. Cook for 30 seconds on a medium heat to brown the other side.

Take off the heat and arrange the mackerel on a serving plate over a bed of cos lettuce and spinach. Pour the dressing over, garnish with the spring onion and serve immediately.

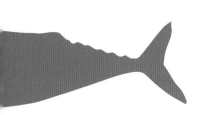

15 mins

5–6 mins

DF

Lacassa Soup – Prawn and Vermicelli Rice Noodle Soup

2 tablespoons rapeseed oil
3 garlic cloves, finely chopped
1 large cayenne chilli, deseeded and finely chopped
2 medium spring onions, sliced into 2cm pieces
170g raw black tiger prawns
2 dried kaffir lime leaves
500ml good-quality hot fish stock
250ml boiling water
100g (3 small blocks) dried vermicelli rice noodles, pre-soaked in warm water for 10 minutes, then drained
pinch of sea salt flakes
pinch of ground white pepper

For the hot and sour fish paste
1 tablespoon Shaohsing rice wine or dry sherry
juice of 1 lime
1 teaspoon sambal oelek or a good chilli sauce
1 teaspoon fermented fish paste
2 tablespoons fish sauce
1 teaspoon soft brown sugar

To serve
small handful of fresh coriander sprigs
lime wedges

Typically eaten on Christmas Eve, a *lacassa* soup is thought to be a Portuguese/Macanese variation of the Malaysian laksa – a coconut-based curry soup. Traditionally, it consists of onions, *balichao* (a fermented fish paste) and shrimp, sautéed in lard. Fresh shellfish stock and vermicelli rice noodles are then added and the dish is seasoned with salt and ground white pepper. Here, I have created my own version by making a pungent spicy paste and combining it with good fish stock to make the perfect salty, fishy, spicy, sour backdrop for fresh tiger prawns and al dente vermicelli rice noodles.

Serves 2 kcal 400 carbs 49.5g protein 23.4g fat 13.2g

Whisk together all the ingredients for the hot and sour fish paste, then set aside.

Heat a wok over a high heat until smoking and add the rapeseed oil. Add the garlic, chilli and spring onions and stir-fry for a few seconds to release their flavours. Add the tiger prawns and stir-fry for a few seconds, then as they start to turn pink, add the hot and sour fish paste and stir quickly. Add the kaffir lime leaves and, in quick succession, pour in the hot stock together with the boiling water. Add the vermicelli rice noodles and stir for 2 minutes, then season with salt and ground white pepper.

Ladle the soup into serving bowls, garnish with coriander sprigs and serve immediately with lime wedges.

10 mins

5-6 mins

DF

Clams in Shrimpy Hot Black Bean Sauce

1 tablespoon rapeseed oil

2 garlic cloves, crushed and finely chopped

knob of fresh root ginger, peeled and grated

2 red chillies, deseeded and finely chopped

1 tablespoon dried shrimp, deep fried and crushed

1 tablespoon fermented salted black beans, rinsed and crushed

500g Japanese littleneck clams (discard any where the shells remain open when tapped)

2 tablespoons Shaohsing rice wine or dry sherry

200ml hot vegetable stock

1 tablespoon low-sodium light soy sauce

1 tablespoon cornflour blended with 2 tablespoons cold water

2 spring onions, sliced into strips and soaked in iced water for 5 minutes to curl

I love clams cooked in a spicy Chinese black bean sauce. The saltiness of the black beans works so well with the sweetness of the clams and the dried fried baby shrimp provide a rich, pungent umami taste. You can turn this into a more substantial dish by adding cooked rice or mung bean glass noodles at the end.

Serves 2 kcal 240 carbs 16.5g protein 18.8g fat 11.4g

Heat a wok over a high heat until smoking and add the rapeseed oil. Add the garlic, ginger, chillies, shrimp pieces and fermented salted black beans and stir-fry for 10 seconds to release their aroma. Add the clams and toss for 10 seconds. As the clam shells start to open, season with the Shaohsing rice wine or dry sherry and discard any clams that remain closed.

Add the hot vegetable stock and bring to the boil, then season with the light soy sauce and stir in the blended cornflour to thicken the sauce.

Transfer to a serving plate, garnish with the spring onion curls and serve.

Wok-seared Miso Sea Bass with Shiitake and Pak Choy

1 tablespoon miso paste

knob of fresh root ginger, peeled and grated

2 x 200g sea bass fillets, skin on

2 tablespoons rapeseed oil

2 tablespoons mirin

1 tablespoon low-sodium light soy sauce

juice of 1 lemon

For the pak choy

1 tablespoon rapeseed oil

1 red chilli, deseeded and finely chopped

4 fresh shiitake mushrooms, cut into 1cm thick slices

200g pak choy leaves

1 tablespoon low-sodium light soy sauce

This is a simple but very tasty meal, perfect with jasmine rice or on its own. You can also use sustainable cod from Icelandic waters, but just cook it for a little longer as it is a meatier fish.

Serves 2 kcal 570 carbs 14.1g protein 43.8g fat 37g

Put the miso paste into a wide, shallow bowl, add a tablespoon of cold water and whisk well, then stir in the grated ginger. Add the sea bass fillets and turn to coat in the mixture.

To cook the pak choy, heat a wok over a high heat until smoking and add 1 tablespoon rapeseed oil. Add the chilli and stir-fry for a few seconds to release its flavour. Add the fresh shiitake slices and toss for a few seconds, then add the pak choy leaves and toss for 1 minute. Season with the light soy sauce, stir, then transfer to a serving plate and cover with foil.

Wipe out the wok and return to the heat, then add the 2 tablespoons rapeseed oil. Add the sea bass fillets, skin side down, and press down with a spatula to prevent the fillets from curling up. Cook for 1–2 minutes until the skin is crisp and the fish has turned opaque, then flip the fish over to brown the other side. Season with the mirin and light soy sauce, then take off the heat and place on top of the pak choy. Drizzle with the lemon juice and serve immediately.

10 mins

5 mins

DF

Sweet Sour Baby Squid with Chilli and Kumquats

1 tablespoon rapeseed oil

2 garlic cloves, finely chopped

knob of fresh root ginger, peeled and grated

1 red chilli, deseeded and finely chopped

250g baby squid, sliced into rings

1/2 teaspoon dark soy sauce

3 tablespoons mirin

2 tablespoons low-sodium light soy sauce

2 tablespoons sweet chilli sauce

juice of 1 lime

large handful of spinach leaves

For the garnish

4 fresh kumquats, finely sliced

small handful of beansprouts

large handful of fresh coriander, finely chopped

This is a quick, fresh-tasting dish that is perfect for summer months. Baby squid is wok-fried with Chinese aromatics, seasoned with sweet mirin, soy and sweet chilli sauce and dressed with zingy lime, kumquats and pungent coriander. Serve on spiralised courgettes for a light low-carb meal.

Serves 2 kcal 280 carbs 26.2g protein 23.1g fat 9.2g

Heat a wok over a high heat until smoking and add the rapeseed oil. Add the garlic, ginger and chilli and stir-fry for a few seconds to release their flavours. Add the squid and toss for 15 seconds, then season with a small drop of dark soy sauce and toss to coat and colour the squid well. Add the mirin, light soy sauce and sweet chilli sauce and season with the lime juice.

Divide the spinach leaves between two plates and pour the stir-fry over. Garnish with the kumquats, beansprouts and coriander and serve immediately.

10 mins

5 mins*

* plus 5 mins in the oven

DF

Chongqing Crispy Prawns

Here I bake the battered prawns rather than frying them, which is a lot lighter and healthier and they still turn out lovely and crispy. Please note, the Sichuan pepper and dried chillies are not for eating but to impart a wonderful numbing spicy hit to the dish. It's traditional to leave them in the dish and eat around them.

Serves 2 kcal 688 carbs 89.4g protein 36.2g fat 23g

1 tablespoon rapeseed oil
1 red chilli, deseeded and finely chopped
large handful of dried 'heaven-facing' chillies
2 tablespoons Sichuan peppercorns
1 red pepper, deseeded and sliced into 2.5cm chunks
1 tablespoon Chinkiang black rice or balsamic vinegar
large handful of roasted peanuts
large pinch of sea salt flakes
large pinch of Chinese five-spice powder
dash of chilli oil
dash of toasted sesame oil
2 spring onions, sliced into strips, soaked in ice cold water to curl

For the prawns
100g potato flour
pinch of sea salt flakes
pinch of ground white pepper
2 eggs, lightly beaten
100g panko breadcrumbs
200g large tiger prawns, shelled, deveined, but tail left on
oil spray

Preheat the oven to 180°C/gas mark 4.

Start with the prawns. Season the potato flour with salt and ground white pepper and put the potato flour, eggs and panko breadcrumbs into three separate bowls. Dust each prawn in the seasoned flour, then dip into the egg and then into the breadcrumbs, ensuring each is coated well. Set on a baking tray. Continue until all the prawns are done in this way, then spray generously with oil, place in the oven and cook for 5 minutes until the prawns are cooked through and golden. Remove and set aside.

Heat a wok over a high heat until smoking and add the rapeseed oil. Add the red chilli, dried chillies and Sichuan peppercorns and stir-fry for a few seconds to release their flavours. Add the red pepper and toss for 10 seconds, then season with the black rice vinegar. Add the roasted peanuts and toss to combine, then add the prawns, toss together and season with a generous pinch of sea salt, the five-spice powder, chilli oil and toasted sesame oil. Add the spring onions and toss for 30 seconds, then serve.

12 mins

5 mins

DF

Steamed Haddock with Wok-fried Honey Roast Ham and Edamame beans

2 haddock fillets, skinned
1 tablespoon Shaohsing rice wine
pinch of sea salt flakes
pinch of ground white pepper
1 tablespoon rapeseed oil
knob of fresh root ginger, peeled and grated
1 red chilli, deseeded and finely chopped
150g honey roast ham, diced into 5mm cubes
250g edamame beans
1 tablespoon Shaohsing rice wine or dry sherry
50ml vegetable stock
1 tablespoon low-sodium light soy sauce
1 teaspoon cornflour blended with 1 tablespoon cold water
1 teaspoon toasted sesame oil
steamed jasmine rice, to serve

This fish dish is very easy to make. You steam cook the haddock in the wok using either a stainless steamer rack or a bamboo steamer and then keep it warm in a low oven while you prepare the delicious wok-fried sauce. The latter is inspired by fava beans with honey roast ham, a popular dish in Hunan. If you prefer, you can substitute a small block of finely diced smoked tofu for the haddock.

Serves 2 kcal 470 carbs 15.8g protein 51.7g fat 20.8g

Place the fish fillets on a heatproof plate and season with Shaohsing rice wine, sea salt and ground white pepper. Place the plate in a bamboo steamer or stainless steel steaming rack, and set over a wok half-filled with boiling water. Cover with the lid, place the wok over a medium heat and steam cook the fish for 6–7 minutes (depending on the thickness of the fillets) until the flesh is opaque white and flakes apart when forked. Carefully remove the fish from the wok, cover with foil and keep warm. Pour away the water from the wok and wipe it clean.

Heat the wok over a high heat until smoking and add the rapeseed oil. Add the ginger and chilli and toss for 10 seconds to release their flavours. Add the ham and cook for 10 seconds, tossing occasionally to sear the edges. Add the edamame beans and toss for 10 seconds, then add the Shaohsing rice wine and vegetable stock. Season to taste with the soy sauce, then stir in the blended cornflour to thicken the sauce. Finally, add a dash of toasted sesame oil, transfer the fish to a serving plate, pour sauce over and serve with steamed jasmine rice.

20 mins*

5 mins

* includes cooking the rice

DF

Smoked Mackerel, Shiitake Mushroom, Bamboo and Goji Berry Rice

1 tablespoon rapeseed oil
knob of fresh root ginger, peeled and grated
120g fresh shiitake mushrooms, rinsed, dried and cut into 5mm slices
2 tablespoons low-sodium light soy sauce
100g French beans, sliced into 5mm rounds
1 x 225g can bamboo shoots, drained and diced into 5 x 5mm pieces
3 tablespoons Shaohsing rice wine or dry sherry
300g cooked jasmine or basmati rice (150g uncooked)
40g roasted peanuts
1 large smoked mackerel fillets, flaked into 2.5cm pieces
1 tablespoon toasted sesame oil
pinch of ground white pepper
small handful of goji berries, rehydrated in warm water for 4 minutes, then drained
1 tablespoon black sesame seeds

This dish reminds me of my grandmother's cooking. The French beans add a nice crunch, and the goji berries provide a pop of sweetness, plus the black sesame seeds give texture and flavour.

Serves 2 kcal 721 carbs 64g protein 27.4g fat 40.6g

Heat a wok over a high heat until smoking and add the rapeseed oil. Add the ginger and stir-fry for a few seconds, then add the shiitake mushrooms and stir-fry for 15 seconds. Season with half the soy sauce and toss for 10 seconds.

Add the French beans and bamboo shoots and toss for 30 seconds, then add the Shaohsing rice wine. Once it has evaporated, add the cooked rice and peanuts and toss together well. Add the smoked mackerel and toss again.

Season to taste with more soy, toasted sesame oil and white pepper. Add the goji berries, sprinkle over black sesame seeds and serve immediately.

Chicken

10 mins

12 mins

DF

Fish Fragrant Chicken and Aubergine

200g boneless chicken thighs, sliced into 1cm strips
pinch of sea salt flakes
pinch of ground white pepper
1 teaspoon cornflour
2 tablespoons rapeseed oil
200g aubergine, sliced into batons
2 garlic cloves, crushed and finely chopped
2.5cm piece of fresh root ginger, peeled and grated
1 medium red chilli, deseeded and finely chopped
1 tablespoon chilli bean sauce
1 tablespoon Shaohsing rice wine or dry sherry
1 spring onion, finely sliced, to garnish

For the sauce
100ml cold vegetable stock
1 tablespoon low-sodium light soy sauce
1 tablespoon Chinkiang black rice or balsamic vinegar
1 tablespoon cornflour

This recipe is an adaptation of one of my favourite Sichuan dishes. It does not contain any fish but is called 'Fish fragrant', or 'Yu Siang', because it uses a good savoury stock. You can also use tofu, minced pork or shiitake mushrooms and serve it with steamed jasmine rice. It's delish and packs a punch!

Serves 2 kcal 365 carbs 21.1g protein 23g fat 21.7g

Place the chicken in a bowl and season with the salt, white pepper and cornflour and stir to combine.

Whisk together all the ingredients for the sauce in a jug, then set aside.

Heat a wok over a high heat and, as the wok starts to smoke, add 1 tablespoon rapeseed oil. Add the aubergine and stir-fry for 5 minutes until softened and brown. During this process, keep adding the 50ml of water in small drops around the edge of the wok to create some steam to help cook and soften the aubergine. When soft and cooked, transfer to a plate and set aside.

Return to the heat and add another tablespoon of rapeseed oil. Add the garlic, ginger, chilli and chilli bean sauce and cook together for a few seconds. Add the chicken strips and cook for 1 minute until they start to turn brown and opaque, then season with the Shaohsing rice wine or dry sherry and stir-fry for 3 minutes until the chicken is cooked all the way through.

Return the aubergines to the wok, pour in the sauce and simmer on a medium heat for 3 minutes. Sprinkle the spring onion over and serve immediately.

10-15 mins

6 mins

DF

Speedy Spicy Singapore Noodles

1 tablespoon rapeseed oil

2 garlic cloves, finely chopped

knob of fresh root ginger, peeled and grated

2 red chillies, deseeded and finely chopped

4 fresh shiitake mushrooms, cut into 5mm slices

120g cooked shredded chicken breast

100g cooked tiger prawns

1 teaspoon ground turmeric

1 tablespoon Shaohsing rice wine or dry sherry

350g cooked vermicelli rice noodles (175g uncooked)

small handful of beansprouts

2 spring onions, finely sliced on the angle

2 tablespoons low-sodium light soy sauce

1 tablespoon oyster sauce

1 egg, lightly beaten

1/2 teaspoon dried red chilli flakes

pinch of freshly ground white pepper

dash of toasted sesame oil

small handful of fresh coriander leaves

This is one of the best Asian fusion dishes as the combination of dried chillies and turmeric with Chinese noodles works every time. Most supermarkets now sell cooked vermicelli noodles in the fresh produce aisle so this dish makes an incredibly easy and speedy meal – great for a casual mid-week supper or even when you're entertaining.

Serves 2 kcal 576 carbs 70.3g protein 38.6g fat 16.6g

Heat a wok over a high heat until smoking and add the rapeseed oil. Add the garlic, ginger and red chillies and cook for a few seconds, then add the mushrooms, chicken and prawns and toss for 20 seconds.

Add the turmeric and cook for another 10 seconds, then add the Shaohsing rice wine or dry sherry in around the edge of the wok. Add the rice noodles, beansprouts and spring onions and toss for 20 seconds, ensuring that all the noodles are coated with the turmeric and the whole dish is uniform yellow in colour. Add a small dash of water around the edge of the wok to help create some steam, then season with the light soy and oyster sauces and toss for 1 minute to combine the seasoning.

Make a well in the centre of the noodles and pour in the beaten egg, then stir to combine and coat the noodles with the egg. Sprinkle with the dried chilli, ground white pepper and toasted sesame oil and give it one last stir.

Transfer to a serving plate, garnish with fresh coriander and serve immediately.

15 mins

6 mins

DF

Chicken and Crispy Vegetables

3 small boneless chicken thighs, sliced into strips
1 teaspoon dark soy sauce
½ teaspoon Chinese five-spice powder
pinch of ground white pepper
1 tablespoon cornflour
1 tablespoon peanut oil
2 garlic cloves, finely chopped
knob of fresh root ginger, peeled and grated
1 tablespoon Shaohsing rice wine or dry sherry
50g carrots, cut into julienne strips
50g baby corn, sliced in half
50g water chestnuts, drained
50g broccoli, cut into florets
50g mangetout
50g beansprouts
1 spring onion, cut at an angle into 2.5cm slices
1 teaspoon toasted sesame oil

For the sauce
50ml cold water
1 tablespoon low-sodium light soy sauce
1 tablespoon oyster sauce
1 tablespoon rice vinegar
1 teaspoon cornflour

The secret to a good stir-fry is very simple – well-seasoned meat together with crispy, crunchy vegetables – and this dish delivers this in spades. The real star is the Chinese five-spice and the dark soy sauce as together they coat the vegetables in a rich, savoury flavour that tastes like a little bit of magic. You can also use pork loin strips instead of chicken if you prefer.

Serves 2 kcal 402 carbs 24.1g protein 31.4g fat 20.7g

Place the chicken strips in a bowl and season with the dark soy sauce, five-spice powder and ground white pepper. Dust with the cornflour and mix well to coat.

Whisk together all the ingredients for the sauce in a jug, then set aside.

Heat a wok over a high heat until smoking and add the peanut oil. Add the garlic and ginger and toss for a few seconds, then add the seasoned chicken strips. Leave for 30 seconds to sear and colour, then flip the strips over, season with the Shaohsing rice wine or dry sherry and stir-fry for 2–3 minutes until the chicken is cooked through and opaque.

Add all the vegetables from the carrots to the spring onion and stir-fry for 2 minutes to wilt the vegetables. Give the sauce a stir, then pour onto the vegetables and cook for 30 seconds until the liquid has thickened and the vegetables are glazed but still crisp. Season with the toasted sesame oil and serve immediately.

15 mins

5 mins

DF

Chicken Teriyaki with Green Peppers

1 tablespoon rapeseed oil
2 garlic cloves, finely chopped
knob of fresh root ginger, peeled and grated
250g boneless chicken thighs, sliced into 1cm x 2.5cm strips
1 tablespoon sake
1 green pepper, deseeded and sliced into 1cm strips
large pinch of freshly ground black pepper

For the sauce
1 tablespoon sake or rice wine
2 tablespoons mirin
2 tablespoons low-sodium light soy sauce
1 teaspoon caster sugar

For the garnish
1 spring onion, finely sliced
pinch of black sesame seeds

I love the Japanese teriyaki marinade as it's super-delicious and the perfect sauce for a fabulous stir-fry. Here, also, the green peppers provide the perfect fresh and crunchy accompaniment. I like using juicy chicken thighs but you can also use a chunky piece of sirloin steak and slice it into strips. Quick, easy and delicious – you'll have dinner on the table in minutes!

Serves 2 kcal 360 carbs 16.2g protein 28.1g fat 18.6g

Whisk together all the ingredients for the sauce in a small jug, then set aside.

Heat a wok over a high heat until smoking and add the rapeseed oil, then add the garlic and ginger and stir-fry for a few seconds to release their flavours. Add the chicken and cook until seared and browned at the edges. Season with the sake and stir-fry for 2 seconds. Add the green pepper and stir-fry for 10 seconds, then pour in the sauce and bring to a simmer. Cook until the sauce starts to reduce and you end up with a slightly sticky shine on the chicken and peppers. Season with a large pinch of freshly ground black pepper, then transfer to a serving plate.

Garnish with the spring onion and black sesame seeds and serve immediately.

5 mins

7 mins

DF

Three-cup Chicken

250g boneless chicken thighs,
   sliced into 1cm x 2.5cm cubes
pinch of sea salt flakes
pinch of ground white pepper
1 tablespoon cornflour
1 tablespoon rapeseed oil
large knob of fresh root
   ginger, peeled and cut into
   large slices
2 garlic cloves, crushed but
   left whole
1 red chilli, sliced into rings
1 tablespoon Shaohsing rice
   wine or dry sherry
50ml low-sodium light soy sauce
50ml toasted sesame oil
1 teaspoon caster sugar
5g Taiwanese nine-pagoda leaf
   basil or Thai sweet basil

This is a classic Taiwanese recipe that is perfect for a quick and speedy supper. It's called Three-cup Chicken because traditionally it uses 1 cup of soy sauce, 1 cup of rice wine and 1 cup of toasted sesame oil – in this recipe there's not quite 1 cup of each but certainly equal measures of all three. If Japan is famous for inventing teriyaki sauce, Taiwan is famous for its Three-cup Chicken sauce. The sweet basil at the end imparts an aniseed aroma and taste, which pairs perfectly with this dish. If you can't get Taiwanese basil, try Thai sweet basil or sweet basil.

Serves 2 kcal 561 carbs 17.2g protein 27.8g fat 42.9g

Place the chicken in a bowl, add the salt and ground white pepper and then dust with the cornflour. Mix well to coat then set aside.

Heat a wok over a high heat until smoking and add the rapeseed oil. Add the ginger slices and fry until crispy and golden, then add the garlic and red chilli and toss for a few seconds to release their flavour. Add the chicken pieces and leave for 10 seconds to sear and colour, then flip them over. Season with Shaohsing rice wine or dry sherry and stir-fry for 2–3 minutes on a high heat until the chicken is almost cooked.

Add the light soy sauce, the toasted sesame oil and sugar and cook for 5 minutes until the liquid has almost evaporated. The chicken should have a dark brown, slightly sticky shine. Add the basil leaves and toss through to wilt, then take off the heat and serve immediately.

15 mins

7 mins

DF

Spicy Lemongrass Chicken with Cashew Nuts

3 small boneless chicken thighs, sliced into 1cm-thick strips
pinch of sea salt flakes
pinch of ground white pepper
1 tablespoon cornflour
1 tablespoon rapeseed oil
1 onion, halved and sliced
1 garlic clove, crushed and finely chopped
knob of fresh root ginger, peeled and grated
1 stalk of lemongrass, sliced into 2.5cm pieces
1 tablespoon Shaohsing rice wine or dry sherry
1 green pepper, deseeded and sliced into julienne strips
100ml hot chicken stock
1 teaspoon soft brown sugar
1 tablespoon low-sodium light soy sauce
1 teaspoon fish sauce
1/2 teaspoon dark soy sauce
2 large spring onions, cut on the angle into 1cm slices
small handful of roasted cashew nuts
10 Thai basil leaves

This is a tasty 'fusion'-style stir-fry – I love mixing Chinese and Thai ingredients for a mash-up of Asian flavours. After all, the Dai people in Thailand minority originated from Yunnan Province in China. Here, I have taken creative license and combined Shaohsing rice wine with flavours of lemongrass, fish sauce and Thai basil. This works wonderfully well and gives a moreish intense umami flavour to the stir-fry.

Serves 2 kcal 439 carbs 25.6g protein 31.6g fat 24.7g

Place the chicken strips in a bowl, season with sea salt and ground white pepper and dust with the cornflour. Mix well to coat, then set aside.

Heat a wok over a high heat until smoking and add the rapeseed oil. Toss in the onion, garlic, ginger and lemongrass and stir-fry for a few seconds to release their flavours. Add the chicken and cook for 10 seconds until seared and browned, then flip the meat over and stir-fry for 2 minutes. As it starts to turn opaque, season and deglaze the wok with the Shaohsing rice wine or dry sherry. Stir-fry for another 1–2 minutes until the chicken is completely cooked through.

Add the green pepper strips and toss for 30 seconds, then add the hot stock, brown sugar, light soy sauce, fish sauce and dark soy sauce and toss in the spring onions and cashew nuts. Cook, stirring to mix well.

Just before serving, add the Thai basil leaves and toss together well.

Chicken with Chinese Curry Sauce

200g chicken breast, skinned and cut into 2.5cm chunks
pinch of sea salt flakes
pinch of ground white pepper
1 tablespoon cornflour
1 tablespoon groundnut oil
1 garlic clove, crushed and finely chopped
knob of fresh root ginger, peeled and grated
1 green chilli, deseeded and finely chopped
½ white onion, sliced
1 tablespoon Shaohsing rice wine or dry sherry
1 small carrot, sliced diagonally into oval pieces
handful of broccoli florets
1 spring onion, finely chopped

For the curry sauce
150ml cold fresh chicken stock
1 star anise
1 teaspoon ground turmeric
½ teaspoon Madras hot curry powder
1 teaspoon brown sugar
1 tablespoon cornflour

This Chinese chicken curry is similar to what you would get from a Chinese takeaway. Mildly spicy and sweet, it's a warm and comforting dish, perfect for winter and delicious with jasmine rice.

Serves 2 kcal 288 carbs 28.2g protein 28.8g fat 7.6g

Place the chicken in a bowl, season with the salt and white pepper and dust with the cornflour. Mix well to coat, then set aside. Whisk together all the ingredients for the curry sauce in a jug, then set aside.

Heat a wok over a high heat until smoking and add the groundnut oil. Add the garlic, ginger, chilli and sliced onion and stir-fry for a few seconds to release their aroma. Add the chicken and let it settle for 10 seconds to sear and brown, then flip it over. Add the Shaohsing rice wine or dry sherry and toss the chicken for 2 minutes until cooked through.

Add the carrot and broccoli and toss for 1 minute, then drizzle a tablespoon of cold water around the edge of the wok to create steam to help cook the vegetables. Pour in the sauce and bring to the boil.

Transfer to a serving plate, garnish with the spring onion and serve immediately.

15 mins

8 mins

DF

Lemon Chicken

1 tablespoon potato flour

1 egg, lightly beaten

200g breadcrumbs or Panko breadcrumbs

250g chicken breast, skinned and butterflied in half

pinch of Chinese five-spice powder

1 teaspoon lemon zest

pinch of dried chilli flakes

pinch of sea salt flakes

pinch of ground black pepper

800ml rapeseed oil

1 spring onion, finely sliced (optional)

For the lemon sauce

1 teaspoon freshly grated root ginger

1 tablespoon Shaohsing rice wine or dry sherry

200ml hot vegetable stock

juice of 1 lemon

1 teaspoon caster sugar

pinch of sea salt flakes

1 teaspoon low-sodium light soy sauce

1 tablespoon cornflour blended with 2 tablespoons cold water

For the garnish and to serve

1 spring onion, finely sliced (optional)

This is a Chinese takeaway classic and delicious served with steamed rice or noodles. It may not be the most straightforward stir-fry recipe, but it was too delicious to leave out. Enjoy!

Serves 2 kcal 658 carbs 99.7g protein 44.5g fat 11.7g

Place the potato flour, beaten egg and breadcrumbs in three separate bowls. Place the chicken breast in a large shallow bowl and season with the five-spice powder, lemon zest, chilli flakes, salt and ground black pepper. Turn the meat to coat well in the seasoning, then dip it first in the potato flour, then in the beaten egg and then in the breadcrumbs, again coating well.

Fill a wok just under half-full with rapeseed oil. Heat the oil to 180°C or until a piece of bread dropped in turns golden in 15 seconds. Using a spider or slotted metal spoon, gently lower the breadcrumbed chicken into the oil and fry for 5 minutes until golden brown. Insert a toothpick into the chicken and check it comes out clean to ensure the chicken breast is cooked through. Drain the chicken on paper towels and keep covered with foil.

To make the lemon sauce, pour the oil from the wok into a heatproof bowl through a sieve. Retain 1 teaspoon of oil in the wok and reheat the wok over a high heat. Add the ginger and stir-fry for 2 seconds, then add the Shaohsing rice wine or dry sherry. Pour in the vegetable stock and bring to a simmer. Add the lemon juice, sugar and sea salt, then season with the light soy sauce. Stir in the blended cornflour to thicken the sauce.

Slice the chicken onto serving plates and pour the lemon sauce over, then garnish with the spring onion, if using. Serve with steamed broccoli or other greens.

DF

Sesame Chicken

1 tablespoon rapeseed oil

2 garlic cloves, crushed and finely chopped

knob of fresh root ginger, peeled and grated

250g boneless chicken thighs, sliced into strips

1 tablespoon sake

1 tablespoon mirin

1 tablespoon low-sodium light soy sauce

1 tablespoon toasted sesame oil

pinch of caster sugar

2 spring onions, finely sliced on the diagonal

2 tablespoons toasted black and white sesame seeds

This is a great savoury, nutty stir-fry that is packed with flavour. You can add beansprouts or blanched greens and toss together or even add thin egg noodles to turn this into a chow mein. Perfect served with steamed broccoli – either on the side or tossed together at the end – and steamed jasmine rice.

Serves 2 kcal 424 carbs 7.3g protein 29.1g fat 30.2g

Heat a wok over a high heat until smoking and add the rapeseed oil. Add the garlic and ginger and toss for a few seconds to release their flavours. Add the chicken strips and leave to sear and brown for 10 seconds, then flip them over.

Add the sake and mirin and toss for a few seconds, then season with the light soy sauce, toasted sesame oil and sugar. Toss to combine well, then add the spring onions and toss again to mix.

Transfer to a plate, sprinkle with the toasted black and white sesame seeds and serve with steamed broccoli and rice.

Oyster Sauce Chicken with Celery and Peanuts

250g boneless chicken thighs, sliced into 1cm strips
pinch of sea salt flakes
pinch of ground white pepper
1 tablespoon cornflour
1 tablespoon rapeseed oil
2 garlic cloves, crushed and finely chopped
1 tablespoon Shaohsing rice wine or dry sherry
2 large celery sticks, sliced on the diagonal into 2.5cm pieces
1 tablespoon low-sodium light soy sauce
1 tablespoon oyster sauce
pinch of dried chilli flakes
a small handful of roasted peanuts
1 teaspoon toasted sesame oil

This is a simple home-cooked dish, no explanations required – easy and delicious, it's a winner! Serve with steamed jasmine rice.

Serves 2 kcal 402 carbs 14.2g protein 30.2g fat 25.6g

Place the chicken in a large bowl, season with the sea salt and ground white pepper and dust with the cornflour. Mix well to coat, then set aside.

Heat a wok over a high heat until smoking and add the rapeseed oil. Add the garlic and toss for a few seconds to release its aroma. Add the chicken and leave for 10 seconds to sear and brown, then flip the pieces over and stir-fry for 2 minutes.

Add the Shaohsing rice wine or dry sherry, then the celery and cook for just under 1 minute until softened but still crisp. Season with the light soy sauce, oyster sauce and chilli flakes and mix well.

Add the roasted peanuts and season with the toasted sesame oil. Stir well, then take off the heat and serve immediately.

15 mins

7 mins

DF

Pineapple Chicken

250g boneless chicken thighs,
    sliced into 1.5cm cubes
pinch of sea salt flakes
pinch of ground black pepper
1 tablespoon cornflour
1 tablespoon rapeseed oil
2 dried chillies, whole
1 tablespoon Shaohsing rice
    wine or dry sherry
½ small pineapple, sliced into
    1.5cm cubes
½ red pepper, deseeded and
    sliced into 1.5cm cubes
small handful of roasted cashew
    nuts (optional)
1 spring onion, finely sliced
handful of fresh coriander
    leaves, to garnish

For the sauce
100ml pineapple juice
1 tablespoon low-sodium light
    soy sauce
1 tablespoon cornflour
juice of 1 lime
1 teaspoon runny honey
¼ teaspoon sriracha chilli sauce

I love this dish because I'm a big fan of fresh, juicy sweet pineapples. This may seem like a long list of ingredients but it's so quick and easy to prepare once you have them all. If you are vegan, you can use smoked tofu instead of chicken and you could also turn this into a chow mein dish by adding cooked egg noodles at the end, if you wish.

Serves 2 kcal 496 carbs 43.1g protein 30.1g fat 24.4g

Place the chicken in a bowl and season with the salt and pepper. Add the cornflour and mix well to coat, then set aside.

Whisk together all the ingredients for the sauce in a small jug, then set aside.

Heat a wok over a high heat and, when the wok starts to smoke, add the rapeseed oil. Add the chillies and fry for a few seconds to release their flavour, then add the chicken pieces and stir-fry for 2–3 minutes. As the chicken starts to turn opaque, add the Shaohsing rice wine or dry sherry and cook for another 2–3 minutes until the chicken is cooked through.

Add the pineapple and red pepper pieces and cook for just under 30 seconds. Pour in the sauce, bring to the boil and simmer until the sauce has reduced, is slightly sticky and has a thicker consistency.

Add the cashew nuts (if using), followed by the spring onion and cook for 20 seconds. Stir together well, then transfer to a serving plate, garnish with fresh coriander and serve immediately.

DF

Satay Chicken Stir-fry with Spicy Coconut Peanut Sauce

250g boneless chicken thighs, sliced into 1cm-thick strips
½ teaspoon ground turmeric
½ teaspoon ground coriander
1 teaspoon ground lemongrass
pinch of sea salt flakes
pinch of ground white pepper
1 tablespoon cornflour
1 tablespoon rapeseed oil
1 tablespoon Shaohsing rice wine or dry sherry
1 tablespoon low-sodium light soy sauce
juice of ½ lime

For the sauce
1 garlic clove, finely chopped
1 medium red chilli, deseeded and finely chopped
1 large shallot, finely chopped
½ teaspoon tamarind paste
½ teaspoon shrimp paste (optional)
1 teaspoon chilli paste or sriracha chilli sauce
3 tablespoons crunchy peanut butter
1 tablespoon runny honey
50ml hot water
150ml reduced fat coconut milk

For the garnish
a handful of beansprouts
1 spring onion, sliced on the diagonal
fresh coriander leaves
lime wedges

This dish is inspired by my love of Indonesian-style satays – especially the spicy peanut sauce they serve with chargrilled skewers. However, here I'm turning it on its head and using the sauce for a delicious stir-fry. There's no need for sauce packets, just storecupboard ingredients and some fresh produce. This dish is delicious with jasmine rice or served on top of chunky egg noodles.

Serves 2 kcal 563 carbs 26.7g protein 34.2g fat 36.6g

Place the chicken in a bowl and season with the turmeric, ground coriander, lemongrass, salt and pepper, then add the cornflour and toss to coat.

Place all the ingredients for the sauce except the hot water and coconut milk in a small food processor and blend to a fine paste. Turn out and loosen with the hot water and stir well to mix, then add the coconut milk and stir again.

Heat a wok over a high heat until smoking and add the rapeseed oil. Add the chicken pieces and leave to settle in the wok for 2 minutes until seared and browned, then flip over. As the chicken starts to brown, add the Shaohsing rice wine or dry sherry and stir-fry for 2–3 minutes until cooked through.

Pour in the sauce and stir together for 30 seconds to release the aroma, then bring to the boil. Season with the light soy sauce and lime juice to taste.

Transfer to a serving plate, top with the beansprouts, spring onion, coriander leaves and lime wedges.

Hoisin Duck with Soy Pomegranate

300g duck breast fillets, skinned and sliced into 2.5cm strips 5mm thick
1 tablespoon cornflour
1 tablespoon groundnut oil
1 garlic clove, crushed and finely chopped
1 tablespoon freshly grated peeled root ginger
1 tablespoon Shaohsing rice wine or dry sherry
3 cavolo nero leaves, washed, trimmed and cut into 1cm slices

For the duck marinade
½ teaspoon Chinese five-spice powder
1 teaspoon toasted sesame oil
½ teaspoon dark soy sauce
pinch of sea salt flakes

For the soy pomegranate sauce
100ml cold vegetable stock
2 tablespoons hoisin sauce
1 teaspoon runny honey
1 tablespoon low-sodium light soy sauce
50ml pomegranate juice
1 tablespoon cornflour

For the garnish and to serve
60g fresh pomegranate seeds
1 spring onion, trimmed and sliced on the diagonal

This is a delicious stir-fry using duck breast fillets. I usually like to serve it for a Chinese-style feast post-Christmas on Boxing Day. There may seem like a long list of ingredients, but I promise it's dead easy.

Serves 2 kcal 439 carbs 38g protein 32.8g fat 18.2g

Whisk together all the ingredients for the marinade in a bowl, then add the duck and turn to coat. Leave to marinate for 10 minutes, then dust with the cornflour.

Whisk together all the ingredients for the soy pomegranate sauce in a jug, then set aside.

Heat a wok over a high heat until smoking and add the groundnut oil. Add the garlic and ginger and stir-fry for a few seconds to release their flavours. Add the duck and let it settle for 10 seconds to sear and brown on one side, then flip it over and season with the Shaohsing rice wine or dry sherry. Add the cavolo nero and toss for 10 seconds until it starts to wilt, then drizzle in 1 tablespoon cold water around the edge of the wok to create some steam to help cook the kale. Toss and cook all together.

Give the soy pomegranate sauce a stir and pour into the wok, then bring to the boil gently, stirring. The sauce should thicken and become glossy.

Remove from the heat and transfer to a serving plate, garnish with the pomegranate seeds and spring onion and serve immediately.

Sichuan Chicken with Baby Courgettes

2 boneless chicken thighs, sliced
thinly on the angle
pinch of sea salt flakes
pinch of ground white pepper
1 tablespoon cornflour
1 tablespoon rapeseed oil
2 small garlic cloves, crushed
and roughly chopped
2.5cm piece of fresh root ginger,
peeled and finely grated
1 large red cayenne chilli,
deseeded and sliced
1 tablespoon Shaohsing rice
wine or dry sherry
200g baby courgettes, cut on the
angle into 5mm slices
1–2 tablespoons cold water

For the Sichuan spicy sauce
50ml cold water
1 teaspoon chilli bean paste
1 tablespoon Chinkiang black
rice or balsamic vinegar
1 tablespoon low-sodium light
soy sauce
½ teaspoon soft brown sugar
1 teaspoon cornflour
1 teaspoon toasted sesame oil

This is a spicy saucy dish that is incredibly moreish and one of my favourite things to cook at home. You can up the game with more vegetables if you wish and add carrots or assorted peppers. Serve with steamed jasmine rice.

Serves 2 kcal 300 carbs 19.9g protein 20.5g fat 15.9g

Whisk together all the ingredients for the Sichuan spicy sauce in a bowl, then set aside.

In another bowl, season the chicken strips with salt and ground white pepper and then dust with the cornflour. Mix to coat well then set aside.

Heat a wok over a high heat until smoking and add the rapeseed oil. Add the garlic, ginger and red chilli and toss for a few seconds to release their flavours. Add the chicken strips and stir-fry for 2 minutes, then as they start to turn brown, add the Shaohsing rice wine or dry sherry. Stir-fry for another 2 minutes until the chicken is tender and cooked through.

Add the courgette slices and toss for 1 minute. Drizzle in a little cold water around the edge of the wok to create steam to help cook the courgettes. Pour in the sauce and stir-fry for 1 minute until the courgettes have softened and the sauce has thickened. Give the mixture a final stir, then take off the heat and serve immediately.

Hot Sweet and Sour Chicken

1 tablespoon rapeseed oil

1 garlic clove, finely chopped

2.5cm piece fresh root ginger, peeled and sliced into matchsticks

2 medium red chillies, deseeded and sliced

250g boneless chicken thighs, sliced into 1cm x 2.5cm strips

1 tablespoon Shaohsing rice wine or dry sherry

250g spiralised courgettes

sprinkle of toasted sesame seeds, to garnish

For the sauce

50ml mirin

1 teaspoon chilli bean paste

2 tablespoons low-sodium light soy sauce

2 tablespoons rice vinegar

2 tablespoons runny honey

This is sweet, spicy, salty and sour – all my favourite flavours in one dish and perfect for a quick mid-week supper. You can toss the spiralised courgettes in to heat through if you prefer, or serve them raw. You can also serve this with steamed greens and jasmine rice. Whichever way you go...enjoy!

Serves 2 kcal 432 carbs 34g protein 30.1g fat 19.7g

Whisk together all the ingredients for the sauce in a bowl, then set aside.

Heat a wok over a high heat until smoking and add the rapeseed oil. Add the garlic, ginger and chillies and toss for a few seconds to release their aroma. Add the chicken and let it settle for 15 seconds to sear and brown, then flip it over and cook for 1 minute. As it starts to brown, add the Shaohsing rice wine or dry sherry and cook for a further 2 minutes until the chicken is cooked through.

Pour in the sauce and stir-fry until the sauce has reduced and is thick and glossy.

Divide the spiralised courgettes between two plates, arrange the chicken on top , sprinkle over the toasted sesame seeds for a nutty garnish and serve immediately.

Pork, beef

& lamb

15 mins

10 mins

DF

Cantonese-style Sweet and Sour Pork

250g pork fillet, cut into
    5mm slices
pinch of sea salt flakes
pinch of ground white pepper
1 egg, lightly beaten
1 tablespoon cornflour
400ml groundnut oil
knob fresh root ginger, peeled
    and grated
2 long dried chillies
1 red pepper, deseeded and
    cut into 2.5cm chunks
1 green pepper, deseeded and
    cut into 2.5cm chunks
1 x 227g can of pineapple chunks
1 tablespoon low-sodium light
    soy sauce
1 tablespoon clear rice vinegar
    or cider vinegar
1/2 teaspoon brown sugar
1 teaspoon cornflour blended
    with 1 tablespoon cold water

To garnish
handful of fresh coriander leaves
1 spring onion, sliced into
    julienne strips and soaked in
    iced water to curl

This is a hugely popular and well recognised dish in Chinese restaurants and my favourite way to cook Cantonese-style Sweet and Sour Pork. The recipe is taken from my book _Chinese Food in Minutes_. Serve with steamed jasmine rice.

Serves 2 kcal 463 carbs 35.2g protein 33.8g fat 22g

Place the pork fillet in a bowl and season with the salt and ground white pepper. Mix the egg and cornflour together to create a batter. Pour over the pork pieces and coat well.

Heat a wok over a high heat and pour in the groundnut oil. Heat until the oil glistens and a small piece of bread dropped in turns golden brown in 15 seconds and floats to the surface. Using a spider or slotted metal spoon, carefully add the pork slices to the oil and fry for 3–4 minutes until golden brown. Using chopsticks or the spider, lift out the meat and place on a plate lined with kitchen paper to drain any excess oil.

Pour the oil from the wok into a heatproof bowl through a sieve and set aside. Retain 1 tablespoon of oil in the wok and return to a high heat until smoking. Add the grated ginger, dried chillies and peppers and quickly stir-fry to stop the ginger from catching. Stir for 2 minutes, then add the pineapple chunks and their juice and bring to the boil. Season with the light soy sauce, vinegar and brown sugar and, as the liquid reduces and simmers, stir in the blended cornflour and cook until the mixture thickens. Return the pork to the wok, stir and toss together well so the pork is covered in the sauce. Serve immediately.

1 hour*

5 mins

*includes initial cooking of pork

DF

Twice-cooked Pork

200g fatty pork belly, skin on

2 tablespoons rapeseed oil

1 tablespoon Shaohsing rice wine or dry sherry

1 teaspoon chilli bean paste

1 teaspoon yellow bean sauce

1 teaspoon fermented salted black beans, rinsed and crushed

2 spring onions or baby leeks, sliced on the diagonal

1 teaspoon dark soy sauce

1 tablespoon low-sodium light soy sauce

pinch of caster sugar

pinch of sea salt flakes

pinch of freshly ground white pepper

300g steamed jasmine rice, to serve

For the pickled cucumber

1 garlic clove, minced with a pinch of caster sugar

1 tablespoon clear rice vinegar or cider vinegar

1 teaspoon chilli bean paste

1 teaspoon chilli oil

1 tablespoon toasted sesame oil

2 small cucumbers, sliced in half lengthways, deseeded, then cut into 1cm strips

1 fresh red cayenne chilli, deseeded and cut into small strips

If the Chinese did fried bacon, this would be it. After the pork belly slices are poached they are placed in the fridge to firm up and then sliced thinly and wok-fried with chilli bean paste, yellow bean paste and soy. The important thing is to slice the meat as finely as you can and then to fry the pork pieces so they are crisp and golden at the edges, Serve with a side of quick pickled cucumbers and plain rice. For a vegan version, use slices of smoked tofu. Truly versatile and delicious.

Serves 2 kcal 692 carbs 56.7g protein 27.3g fat 41g

For the pork, pour 700 cold water into a large pan, add the pork and bring to the boil, then boil for 30 minutes. Drain and leave to cool. When cold, transfer the meat to the fridge for 1 hour to firm up.

Meanwhile, make the pickled cucumber. Combine the garlic, sugar, vinegar, chilli bean paste, chilli oil and sesame oil in a bowl. Add the cucumber strips and leave to marinate in the fridge for 20 minutes.

Remove the cucumbers from the fridge and add the fresh chilli. Remove the pork from the fridge and cut into 5mm thick slices.

Heat a wok over a high heat until smoking and add the rapeseed oil, then the pork (or tofu). As the pork starts to brown, add the Shaohsing rice wine or dry sherry and cook until the pork has browned and the skin is slightly crisp. Add the chilli bean paste, yellow bean sauce and fermented black beans and stir-fry for 1 minute. Add the spring onions or leeks and stir-fry for just under 1 minute until well mixed. Stir in both soy sauces and the sugar, then season with salt and ground white pepper.

To serve, place a spoonful of rice onto each plate and spoon the pork (or tofu) over the top, then add the pickled cucumber alongside it.

10 mins

7-8 mins

DF

Zhajiang Noodles

2 tablespoons rapeseed oil

1 tablespoon finely chopped garlic

1 tablespoon finely chopped root ginger

2 tablespoons diced baby leeks

1 teaspoon Sichuan peppercorns

200g smoked lardons, finely diced

1 tablespoon Shaohsing rice wine or dry sherry

1 tablespoon fragrant oil (see tip)

1 teaspoon dark soy sauce

150ml hot chicken or pork stock

1 tablespoon tian mian jiang or hoisin sauce

1 tablespoon yellow bean paste or miso paste

For the noodles

1 tablespoon sesame oil

1 teaspoon dried chilli sauce laced with chilli oil

200g plain wheat flour or egg noodles, cooked, drained and tossed with 1 teaspoon toasted sesame oil

For the garnish

2 small red radishes, sliced into matchsticks

1/2 cucumber, deseeded and sliced into matchsticks

1 spring onion, finely chopped

'Zhajiang mein' means 'mixed sauce noodle' and is a classic Beijing dish that is made with fresh hand-pulled noodles. There are many different variations, and some are saucier than others, but I prefer the traditional Zhajiang noodle, which is slightly drier. I also like to add minced garlic as well as the customary leeks, ginger, Shaohsing rice wine, Sichuan peppercorns and chilli oil. Here, I have also used smoked lardons instead of traditional belly pork (known as the 'five layers of heaven', a reference to the skin, fat, meat, fat, skin) because of their smoky salty cured flavour. The trick is to dry-fry them in the wok until the fat is slightly crispy.

Serves 2   kcal 697   carbs 39.3g   protein 25.3g   fat 49.7g

Start with the noodles. Divide the sesame oil and chilli sauce between two serving bowls. Place the cooked noodles in the bowls, toss in the oil and sauce and set aside.

Heat a wok over a high heat until smoking and add the rapeseed oil. Add the garlic, ginger, leeks and Sichuan peppercorns and toss for a few seconds, then add the lardons and stir-fry for 1 minute. Add the Shaohsing rice wine or dry sherry, the fragrant oil and dark soy sauce and stir-fry for 1 minute. Add the stock, tian mian jiang or hoisin sauce and the yellow bean paste or miso and toss together well. Cook for 2 minutes, stirring until the pork is cooked.

Divide the pork mixture between the two bowls of noodles and garnish with the radish and cucumber matchsticks. Sprinkle with the spring onion and serve immediately. To eat, toss and mix all the ingredients together well.

> **CHING'S TIP**
> Heat 5 tablespoons of groundnut oil. Add a pinch of salt, 1 tablespoon grated ginger and 1 tablespoon finely chopped spring onion, cook for 1 minute then strain the oil into a glass jar. Keep for 5 days in a cool place.

My Posh Yangzhou Fried Rice

2 tablespoons rapeseed oil

3 eggs, lightly beaten

4 fresh shiitake mushrooms, finely diced

50g cooked fresh baby shrimp

50g cooked honey roast ham or Chinese roast pork, diced

300g cooked jasmine rice (150g uncooked)

100g fresh white crabmeat

1 tablespoon low-sodium light soy sauce

1 tablespoon toasted sesame oil

pinch of sea salt flakes

pinch of ground white pepper

1 spring onion, finely sliced, to garnish

chilli sauce, to serve (optional)

This is a beautiful rich fried-rice dish that is perfect for entertaining. However, you can dress it up or down and even use leftovers, if you like. It was invented by Yang Shu, a Sui dynasty government official in the late sixth century, and traditionally the egg is added with the rice and coats each grain. However, I love my eggs scrambled so that golden pieces sit next to smoked Chinese ham, shiitake mushrooms, shrimp and crabmeat. It seems 'posh'-er that way!

Serves 2 kcal 576 carbs 49.6g protein 33.9g fat 28.2g

Heat a wok over a high heat until smoking, then add 1 tablespoon rapeseed oil. Pour in the beaten eggs and leave to settle for 1–2 minutes, then, using a wooden spoon, stir to lightly scramble it. Transfer to a plate and set aside.

Return the wok to the heat and add the remaining rapeseed oil. Add the mushrooms, baby shrimp and honey roast ham or Chinese roast pork and toss for 30 seconds. Add the rice and mix well until the rice has broken down.

Return the scrambled eggs to the wok, add the crabmeat and season with the light soy sauce, sesame oil, salt and white pepper to taste. Toss well to ensure the seasoning has coated all the rice grains evenly.

Garnish with sliced spring onion and serve immediately with some chilli sauce on the side (if you like).

20 mins

5 mins

DF

Spicy Chinese Sausage, Egg and Chinese Chives

1 tablespoon rapeseed oil
pinch of sea salt flakes
1 garlic clove, finely chopped
50g cooked Chinese sausage or chorizo, finely chopped
small handful of dried Chinese shrimp, soaked in warm water for 20 minutes, drained and roughly chopped
1 tablespoon Shaohsing rice wine or dry sherry
1 teaspoon pickled chillies, finely chopped, or chilli sauce
bunch of Chinese chives or spring onions, sliced into 5cm pieces
3 eggs, lightly beaten
1 tablespoon low-sodium light soy sauce
1 teaspoon toasted sesame oil

This is a traditional recipe that my grandmother used to make for me with dried Taiwanese sausages, made from 50 per cent pork meat and 50 per cent pork belly fat, salt and sugar and then wind-dried. The closest alternative you can get to these are dried Cantonese-style *lap chong* sausages, which need to be pre-cooked by boiling them in water for 15 minutes. However, if you can't get them, use chorizo or smoked bacon lardons, for a spicy, salty fusion stir-fry. Either way, it will taste delicious.

Serves 2 kcal 345 carbs 2.5g protein 30.4g fat 23.8g

Heat a wok over a high heat until smoking and add the rapeseed oil. Add the sea salt and let it dissolve in the hot oil. Add the garlic and chopped Chinese sausage or chorizo, followed by the dried shrimp pieces and stir-fry for 1 minute until slightly crisp. Season with the Shaohsing rice wine or dry sherry, then add the pickled chillies or chilli sauce, the Chinese chives or spring onions and toss for 1 minute until the chives start to wilt.

Make a small space in the middle of the wok and add the beaten eggs, then stir to scramble them. Season with the light soy sauce and toasted sesame oil and toss together.

Transfer to a serving plate and serve immediately.

8 mins

6 mins

DF

Minced Soy Pork with String Beans

1 tablespoon rapeseed oil

2 garlic cloves, crushed and finely chopped

1 red chilli, deseeded and finely chopped

300g minced lean pork

½ teaspoon Chinese five-spice powder

1 teaspoon dark soy sauce

1 tablespoon Shaohsing rice wine or dry sherry

200g string or French beans, cut on the angle into 2.5cm slices

50ml cold vegetable stock

1 tablespoon low-sodium light soy sauce

1 teaspoon cornflour blended with 1 tablespoon cold water

pinch of ground black pepper

1 teaspoon toasted sesame oil

I first tasted this dish in Beijing, where Pork and String Beans is a very popular example of home-style cooking. It was cooked for me by a lady who lived down a traditional Beijing *hutong* (a narrow alley) and she used slivers of pork and no cornflour so the dish was quite oily but very delicious. This is my take on it and I hope you give it a try. Perfect served with jasmine rice or you can toss in cooked noodles or your choice.

Serves 2 kcal 298 carbs 8.8g protein 35.8g fat 13.7g

Heat a wok over a high heat until smoking and add the rapeseed oil. Add the garlic and chilli and toss for a few seconds to release their flavours. Add the pork and let it settle in the wok for 30 seconds to brown and sear, then stir-fry for 1 minute. Add the five-spice powder and season with the dark soy sauce. Toss until the pork turns a rich brown colour, then season and deglaze the wok with the Shaohsing rice wine or dry sherry.

Add the beans and toss for 2 minutes. Add the vegetable stock and bring to the boil, then season with the light soy sauce and stir in the blended cornflour to give the dish a shine and gloss. Add a pinch of ground black pepper and season with the toasted sesame oil.

Take off the heat and serve immediately.

10 mins

6 mins

DF

Spring Onion Porky Potatoes

pinch of sea salt flakes

300g potatoes, peeled and cut into thin matchsticks

2 tablespoons rapeseed oil

1 tablespoon finely chopped garlic

knob of fresh root ginger, peeled and grated

1 red chilli, deseeded and finely chopped

250g lean minced pork

1 tablespoon Shaohsing rice wine or dry sherry

1/2 teaspoon dark soy sauce

1 tablespoon oyster sauce

1 tablespoon low-sodium light soy sauce

3 spring onions, finely chopped

1 teaspoon toasted sesame oil

large pinch of ground black pepper

1 teaspoon chilli oil

This comforting dish is my take on pork hash. You could easily turn it into a delicious brunch by adding a few fried or poached eggs. Great for any weekend – and especially for a hangover!

Serves 2 kcal 429 carbs 34g protein 31.7g fat 19.4g

Pour 600ml cold water into a bowl, add the sea salt, then soak the potatoes in the salted water for 5 minutes. Drain and set aside.

Heat a wok over a high heat until smoking and add 1 tablespoon rapeseed oil. Add the garlic, ginger and red chilli and stir-fry for a few seconds to release their flavour. Add the potatoes and fry for 2 minutes until golden and crisp. Push the ingredients in the wok to one side, add another tablespoon of rapeseed oil and wait for the oil to heat up. Add the minced pork and let it settle for 30 seconds to crisp up and brown. Once the mince starts to sear, add the Shaohsing rice wine or dry sherry, followed by the dark soy sauce, then toss all the ingredients together for another 30 seconds. Add the oyster sauce and light soy sauce and toss again to combine.

Add the spring onions and stir-fry until they have softened but still retain a little bite. Season with the toasted sesame oil, ground black pepper and chilli oil. Stir again, then transfer to a serving plate.

10 mins

7 mins

DF

Ginger Pork and Chinese Broccoli

1 tablespoon rapeseed oil

knob of fresh root ginger, peeled and sliced into matchsticks

1 tablespoon Shaohsing rice wine or dry sherry

200g Chinese broccoli (gai lan), or tenderstem broccoli, cut on the angle into 2.5cm slices

1 teaspoon chilli bean paste

2 tablespoons low-sodium light soy sauce

1 teaspoon clear rice vinegar

1 teaspoon toasted sesame oil

For the pork

300g pork loin steak, sliced into 2.5cm flat strips

pinch of sea salt flakes

pinch of ground white pepper

1 tablespoon cornflour

If you can find a Chinese/Asian grocer near you that stocks fresh 'gai lan' (also known as Chinese broccoli), it will make this dish dreamy. The sweet crunchy stems of the broccoli pair so well with the spicy-gingery-oyster-soy flavours of this dish. If you can't find Chinese gai lan, use tenderstem broccoli – it won't be the same but it will still be delicious. Perfect served with rice or cooked noodles.

Serves 2 kcal 474 carbs 15.3g protein 44.6g fat 26.3g

Combine all the ingredients for the pork in a bowl, then set aside.

Heat a wok over a high heat until smoking and add the rapeseed oil. Add the ginger and toss for 5 seconds, then add the pork pieces and leave to settle in the wok for 10 seconds to brown and sear. Flip the pork over and cook for 30 seconds. Season with the Shaohsing rice wine or dry sherry and toss until all the pork is cooked through.

Add the broccoli, toss for 1 minute, then drizzle in 1 tablespoon cold water around the edges of the wok to create some steam to help it cook. Season with the chilli bean paste, light soy sauce, vinegar and toasted sesame oil and toss to mix well. Transfer to a serving plate and serve immediately.

10 mins

6 mins

DF

Cheat Char Siu Pork with Pak Choy

1 tablespoon rapeseed oil

2 garlic cloves, crushed and finely chopped

knob of fresh root ginger, peeled and grated

1 tablespoon Shaohsing rice wine or dry sherry

200g pak choy leaves, sliced in half on the diagonal

For the pork

250g pork fillet, cut into 5mm slices

½ teaspoon dark soy sauce

1 teaspoon hoisin

1 teaspoon runny honey

pinch of sea salt flakes

pinch of ground white pepper

1 tablespoon cornflour

For the sauce

50ml cold water

1 tablespoon low-sodium light soy sauce

1 teaspoon hoisin sauce

½ teaspoon yellow bean paste or miso paste

I love the flavour of char siu pork but it takes some time to roast and if you want dinner in minutes then this is my cheat char siu pork stir-fry. Serve with steamed jasmine rice.

Serves 2 kcal 323 carbs 19g protein 30.1g fat 14.2g

Place all the ingredients for the pork except the cornflour in a bowl and turn to coat the meat evenly. Dust with the cornflour and set aside.

Whisk together all the ingredients for the sauce in a jug, then set aside.

Heat a wok over a high heat until smoking and add the rapeseed oil. Add the garlic and ginger and stir-fry for a few seconds to release their flavours. Add the pork fillet and let it settle for 10 seconds to sear and brown, then flip it over. Add the Shaohsing rice wine or dry sherry and toss for another 5 seconds. Add the pak choy leaves, then drizzle in 1 tablespoon cold water around the edge of the wok to create some steam to help it cook. Toss for 30 seconds to wilt the leaves, then pour in the sauce and toss again.

Transfer to a serving plate and serve immediately.

12
mins*

5
mins

* includes marinating
the pork

DF

Salty Fried Yellow Bean Pork with Baby Corn and Sugarsnap Peas

250g pork loin, sliced against the grain into 1cm x 2.5cm strips

1 teaspoon cornflour

1 tablespoon rapeseed oil

1 tablespoon Shaohsing rice wine or dry sherry

100g baby sweetcorn, sliced in half on the diagonal

150g sugarsnap peas

1 tablespoon low-sodium light soy sauce

For the marinade

2 garlic cloves, crushed and finely chopped

knob of fresh root ginger, peeled and grated

1 teaspoon yellow bean paste or miso paste

pinch of ground black pepper

A delicious savoury, porky stir-fry with crisp, crunchy vegetables. The black pepper complements the salty yellow bean paste. Perfect with jasmine rice.

Serves 2 kcal 388 carbs 11.3g protein 38g fat 21.1g

Whisk together all the ingredients for the marinade in a bowl, add the pork and leave to marinate for 10 minutes, then dust with the cornflour.

Heat a wok over a high heat until smoking and add the rapeseed oil. Add the pork and let it settle for 10 seconds to sear and brown, then flip it over and stir-fry for 1 minute. Season with the Shaohsing rice wine or dry sherry, then add the baby corn and sugarsnap peas and toss for 1 minute, adding a dash of water around the edge of the wok to create some steam to help cook the vegetables.

Season with the light soy sauce and serve.

Beef and Kimchi Water Chestnuts

350g sirloin steak, fat trimmed off, sliced against the grain into 1cm thick strips
pinch of sea salt flakes
pinch of ground black pepper
1 tablespoon cornflour
1 tablespoon rapeseed oil
knob of fresh root ginger, grated
200g shop-bought kimchi, drained but 1 tablespoon of liquid reserved
50g water chestnuts, sliced into round coins
1–2 tablespoons low-sodium light soy sauce
1 teaspoon clear rice vinegar or cider vinegar
1 teaspoon chilli oil
2 spring onions, sliced on the angle, to garnish

This is a marriage made in wok heaven. The combination of delicious savoury beef slices paired with the punchy Korean fermented cabbage, kimchi, is out of this world. Traditionally, it's frowned upon to stir-fry kimchi, but I think it's worth going against the rules for this one. The pungent, spicy kimchi complements the meaty beef so well; a simple but elegant dish, perfect for foodie friends.

Serves 2 kcal 378 carbs 16.7g protein 43.2g fat 15.3g

Place the beef strips in a bowl, season with salt and ground black pepper and dust with the cornflour.

Heat a wok over a high heat until smoking and add the rapeseed oil. Add the ginger and toss for a few seconds, then add the beef strips. Sear them on one side until brown, then turn the strips and stir-fry for 1 minute.

Add the kimchi and water chestnuts and toss together, then season with light soy sauce to taste, the vinegar, chilli oil and reserved liquid from the kimchi. Toss gently once more, then garnish with the spring onions and serve.

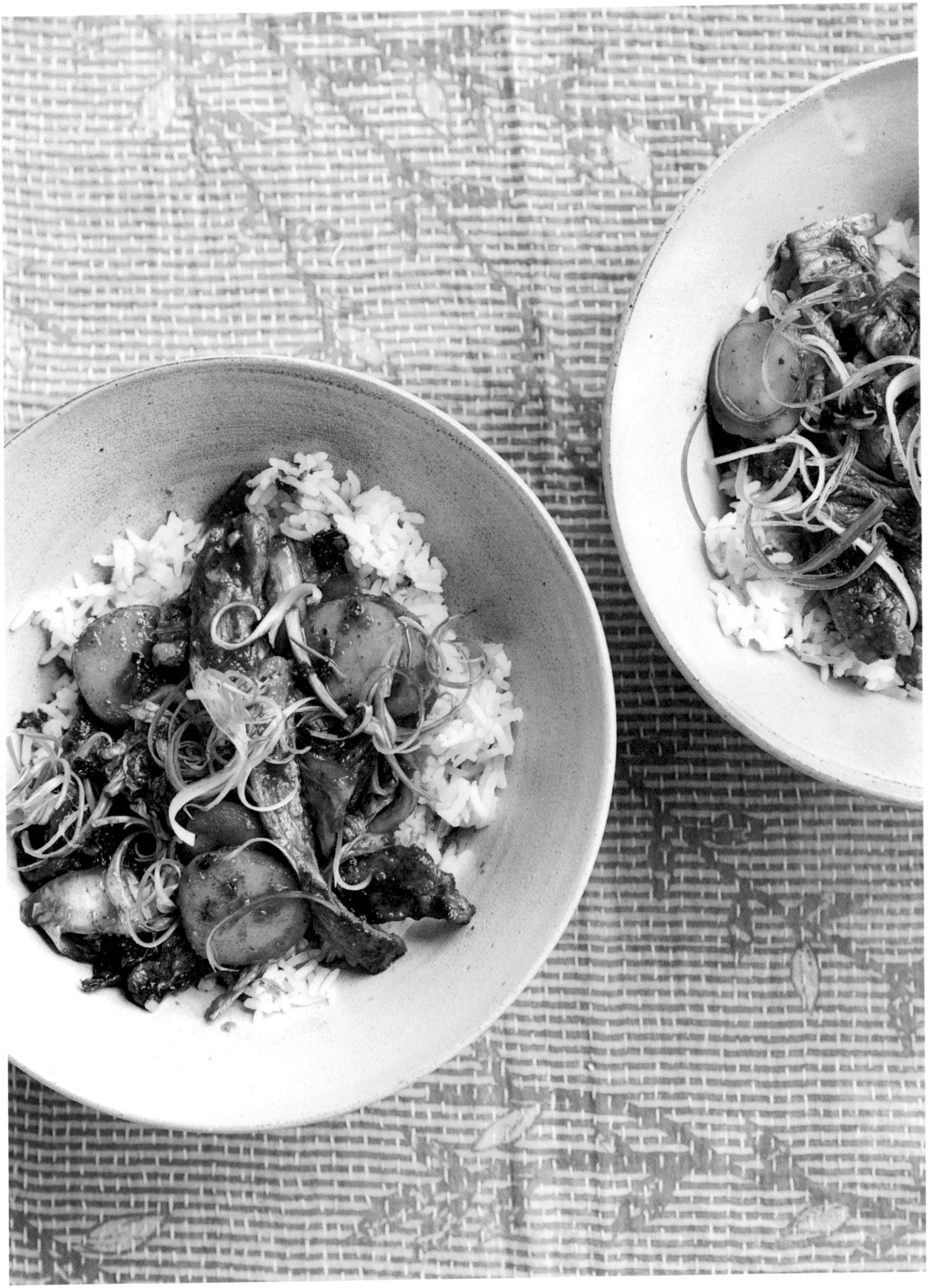

15 mins

5 mins

DF

Thai-style Orange Beef

1 tablespoon rapeseed oil
1 large red onion, finely sliced
   into wedges
1 stalk of lemongrass, finely
   grated
1 red chilli, deseeded and sliced
pinch of ground black pepper

For the beef
1/2 teaspoon Chinese five-spice
   powder
2 x 200g sirloin steaks, fat
   trimmed off, sliced into
   1cm thick strips
pinch of sea salt flakes
pinch of ground black pepper
1 tablespoon cornflour

For the sauce
1 tablespoon low-sodium light
   soy sauce
1 tablespoon fish sauce
1 teaspoon caster sugar
juice of 1 large orange
juice of 1 lime
1 tablespoon cornflour

For the garnish and to serve
2 spring onions, finely sliced
small handful of fresh mint
   leaves
small handful of fresh coriander
   leaves
watercress leaves, to serve
sriracha chilli sauce (optional)

I love the sweet, spicy, pungent flavours of Thai cuisine and this dish is inspired by the beautiful freshness of a Thai Beef Salad and the delicious sticky sweetness of Chinese Orange Beef. They work perfectly together. Add cooked wide rice noodles at the end, if you like, and toss through some cashews for a protein-rich crunch.

Serves 2 kcal 476 carbs 36.4g protein 51g fat 15.1g

Place all the ingredients for the beef in a bowl and toss together, then set aside.

Whisk together all the ingredients for the sauce in a jug, and stir well to dissolve the sugar. Set aside.

Heat a wok over a high heat until smoking and add the rapeseed oil. Add the red onion and stir-fry for 10 seconds until it starts to soften. Add the grated lemongrass and red chilli and toss for a few seconds, then add the beef and sear and brown for 10 seconds. Flip the beef over and toss with the rest of the ingredients for 20 seconds until the beef is coloured and seared on the outside but is still medium on the inside (cook for another minute if you want it well done).

Pour in the sauce and toss for 30 seconds until the beef is well-coated and has absorbed the flavours in the pan. Season with ground black pepper.

Take off the heat immediately and transfer to a serving plate. Garnish with the spring onions, fresh herbs and watercress and toss at the table before eating. If you like a little extra spice, serve with a side of your favourite chilli sauce.

10 mins

5 mins

DF

Sizzling Sichuan Water-cooked Beef

250g beef fillet, fat trimmed
    off, cut into wafer-thin 5cm
    squares (see page 194)
pinch of sea salt flakes
pinch of ground white pepper
1 tablespoon cornflour
1 tablespoon rapeseed oil
2 garlic cloves, crushed and
    finely chopped
knob of fresh root ginger, peeled
    and grated
1 red chilli, deseeded and finely
    chopped
4 whole dried red chillies
150g fresh beansprouts
1 tablespoon Shaohsing rice
    wine or dry sherry
1 tablespoon chilli oil
50ml vegetable oil
3 spring onions, cut on the angle
    into 2.5cm slices
1–2 tablespoons toasted whole
    Sichuan peppercorns

For the sauce
200ml cold chicken stock
1 tablespoon chilli bean paste
1 tablespoon low-sodium light
    soy sauce
1 teaspoon toasted sesame oil
1 tablespoon cornflour

This is my take on the Sichuan classic 'Shui Tzeng Niu Rou' – Water-cooked Beef. There are many variations but I first learnt this dish from a wok master at The New World Restaurant while filming a Chinese New Year segment in London's Chinatown. Although it was a dim sum restaurant, they served other classic Chinese dishes such as this. I didn't get to take the recipe down but I couldn't forget it – it was mesmerising to watch the wok dance that took place. If you are afraid of heat, you can tone down the use of Sichuan peppercorns, but they do impart a delicious numbing heat that is highly addictive.

Serves 2 kcal 634 carbs 26.2g protein 32.9g fat 46.1g

Season the beef with salt and ground white pepper and dust with the cornflour. Whisk together all the ingredients for the sauce in a jug, then set aside.

Heat a wok over a high heat until smoking and add the rapeseed oil. Add the garlic, ginger, red chilli and dried chillies and stir-fry for a few seconds to release their flavours. Add the beansprouts and toss for 5 seconds, then season with the Shaohsing rice wine or dry sherry and the chilli oil.

Pour in the sauce and toss to combine well, then bring to the boil and transfer to a heatproof serving dish.

Wipe out the wok, then place back on the heat, add the vegetable oil and heat to 180°C using a thermometer or until a piece of bread dropped in turns golden brown in 15 seconds. Take off the heat.

Place the spring onions and raw beef slices in the serving dish on top of the beansprouts and sprinkle the Sichuan peppercorns over. Taking care, pour the sizzling hot oil over the top to cook the beef and fry the peppercorns and spring onions. Serve immediately.

20* mins

6 mins

* includes cooking the rice

DF

Beef and Spinach Fried Rice

2 tablespoons rapeseed oil
1 garlic clove, crushed and
    finely chopped
200g spinach leaves
300g cooked basmati rice
    (150g uncooked)
1 tablespoon low-sodium light
    soy sauce
1 teaspoon oyster sauce
1 tablespoon toasted sesame oil
pinch of ground white pepper

For the beef
100g beef sirloin steak, fat
    trimmed off, sliced into
    thin strips
knob of fresh root ginger, peeled
    and grated
pinch of sea salt flakes
pinch of ground white pepper
1 tablespoon Shaohsing rice
    wine or dry sherry

If you have some cooked basmati rice to hand, this dish is incredibly quick to make. If you want to make it carb-free then omit the rice and add some tenderstem broccoli or Chinese leaf to make the dish go further.

Serves 2 kcal 429 carbs 43.7g protein 19.4g fat 20.7g

Combine all the ingredients for the beef in a bowl, then set aside.

Heat a wok over a high heat until smoking and add 1 tablespoon rapeseed oil. Add the garlic and stir-fry for a few seconds to release its flavour, then add the spinach and cook for 5 seconds. Tip in the cooked rice and toss with the spinach for 30 seconds.

Push the rice to one side, then heat up the centre of the wok and pour in the remaining rapeseed oil. Add the beef and let it brown and sear for 10 seconds, then flip it over. Stir-fry until all the beef has coated the rice, then season with the light soy sauce, oyster sauce and toasted sesame oil. Sprinkle with some ground white pepper and serve immediately.

CHING'S TIP
Work quickly so the spinach doesn't become mush.

Spicy Ponzu Beef

1 tablespoon rapeseed oil

2 garlic cloves, crushed and
   finely chopped

1 red chilli, sliced into rings

300g sirloin beef, fat trimmed
   off, cut into 1cm thick slices

1 tablespoon mirin

200g mixed leaves (cos, spinach,
   watercress, wild rocket)

For the dressing

1 tablespoon low-sodium light
   soy sauce

juice of 1 lemon

pinch of caster sugar

For the garnish

sprinkling of bonito flakes

1 spring onion, finely sliced

I love super easy and tasty stir-fried dishes like this, which can be served with a plate of vibrant greens for a delicious supper. If you can, try to get hold of bonito (wood-smoked tuna flakes) from a Japanese or Chinese supermarket as it will impart a smoky sweet flavour to the beef.

Serves 2 kcal 295 carbs 7.8g protein 37.1g fat 12.8g

Whisk together all the ingredients for the dressing in a jar, then set aside.

Heat a wok over a high heat until smoking and add the rapeseed oil. Add the garlic and chilli and toss for a few seconds to release their flavours. Add the beef slices and leave for 10 seconds to sear and brown, then flip them over. Toss for 15 seconds (for medium well done) or 1 minute (for well done). Season with the mirin.

Divide the salad leaves between two plates. Spoon the beef out on top of the leaves, drizzle with the dressing and garnish with the bonito flakes and spring onion, then serve.

Chilli Peanut Lamb

1 tablespoon rapeseed oil

4 whole dried chillies

½ teaspoon ground dry-toasted
   Sichuan peppercorns

250g lamb fillet, sliced into
   thin strips

1 tablespoon Shaohsing rice
   wine or dry sherry

drizzle of toasted sesame oil

dash of chilli oil

handful of dry roasted peanuts

small handful of fresh coriander
   leaves, finely chopped
   (optional)

For the sauce

1 teaspoon chilli bean paste

1 tablespoon crunchy peanut
   butter

1 tablespoon low-sodium light
   soy sauce

1 tablespoon Chinkiang black
   rice vinegar or balsamic
   vinegar

50ml cold water

1 teaspoon cornflour

Here, fine lamb pieces are tossed in a spicy chilli peanut sauce. The result is an addictive, spicy dish that will leave you wanting more. Perfect served with steamed greens and steamed jasmine rice.

Serves 2 kcal 412 carbs 10.4g protein 31.4g fat 27.8g

Whisk together all the ingredients for the sauce in a small jug, then set aside.

Heat a wok over a high heat and add the rapeseed oil. When the wok is smoking, add the dried chillies and ground Sichuan peppercorns and toss for a few seconds. Add the lamb strips and leave to sear on one side for 3 seconds, then flip them over. As the meat starts to turn brown, add the Shaohsing rice wine or dry sherry.

Give the sauce a stir, then pour into the wok and mix well for 5 seconds. Once the sauce thickens and gives a shine to the lamb, drizzle with some toasted sesame oil and chilli oil and toss through some dry roasted peanuts and finely chopped coriander.

Take off the heat and transfer to a serving plate.

20 mins*

5 mins

* includes marinating the beef

DF

Korean Beef Bulgogi Stir-fry

300g sirloin steak, fat trimmed off, sliced against the grain into wafer-thin 5cm pieces (see Tip)
1 tablespoon rapeseed oil
1/2 white onion, cut into half-moon slices
1 tablespoon Shaohsing rice wine or dry sherry
1 green pepper, deseeded and cut into 2.5cm chunks
pinch of Korean gochugaru chilli flakes
pinch of cracked black pepper
2 spring onions, finely sliced on the angle

For the marinade
2 garlic cloves, finely grated
2 tablespoons low-sodium light soy sauce
1 teaspoon Korean gochujang chilli paste
1 teaspoon clear rice wine vinegar
1/2 teaspoon sugar
1 teaspoon pure sesame oil

To garnish and to serve
sprinkle of toasted white sesame seeds, (optional)

I love the flavours of Beef Bulgogi – punchy, savoury and sweet with heady hints of garlic and sesame. In the classic Korean dish, the beef is marinated and cooked on a hot table-top hibachi grill, but I marinate the beef and wok it with onions and green peppers. I've taken a bit of creative license here by adding the Korean gochujang chilli paste – and why not, it's delicious! Perfect served with steamed greens and rice.

Serves 2 kcal 323 carbs 8.7g protein 37.9g fat 15.4g

Whisk together all the ingredients for the marinade in a bowl. Pour over the beef slices and leave to marinate for 10 minutes.

Heat a wok over a high heat until smoking and add the rapeseed oil. Toss in the white onion and stir-fry for 20 seconds until golden and seared at the edges, then add the marinated beef and stir-fry for 5 seconds to sear the edges. Add the Shaohsing rice wine or dry sherry and toss in the green pepper pieces. Stir-fry on a high heat until all the liquid has evaporated, the green peppers are al dente but have softened and the beef is cooked through but still tender. Season with the chilli flakes and black pepper, then take off the heat and stir in the spring onions.

Transfer to a serving plate immediately and sprinkle with the toasted sesame seeds (if you like).

> **CHING'S TIP**
> For wafer-thin slices, wrap the beef in clingfilm and freeze until firm (but not rock hard). Once firm, slice the beef thinly across the grain.

20 mins

5 mins

DF

Xian Lamb with Stir-fried Potatoes

250g organic lamb fillet, sliced into 2cm chunks
120g new potatoes, unpeeled, cut into chunks
1 tablespoon rapeseed oil
2 small red shallots, sliced
1 tablespoon Shaohsing rice wine or dry sherry
1 teaspoon chilli bean paste
100ml hot vegetable stock
1 tablespoon low-sodium light soy sauce
1 tablespoon cornflour blended with 1 tablespoon cold water
1 spring onion, finely sliced

For the spice paste
¼ teaspoon chilli powder
½ teaspoon ground cumin
½ teaspoon ground turmeric
½ teaspoon medium curry powder
½ teaspoon fennel seeds

This spiced lamb stir-fry with potatoes is a Chinese fusion-style stir-fry recipe inspired by my visit to Xian in 2012. The spices are borrowed from Central China and the chilli bean paste from Sichuan (Western China). Delicious with jasmine rice or some flatbread.

Serves 2 kcal 337 carbs 22g protein 27.8g fat 16.5g

Combine all the ingredients for the spice paste in a bowl, add the lamb and turn to coat in the paste. Leave to marinate for 20 minutes. Meanwhile, boil the potatoes.

Heat a wok over a high heat until smoking and add the rapeseed oil. Add the shallots and stir-fry for a few seconds to release their flavour. Add the marinated lamb and let it settle in the wok for 10 seconds, then flip it over and stir-fry for 20 seconds.

Add the Shaohsing rice wine or dry sherry. Add the cooked potatoes and the chilli bean paste and stir-fry for a few seconds. Add the stock and season with the light soy sauce. Bring to a simmer, then stir in the blended cornflour to thicken the sauce. As soon as the sauce bubbles and the ingredients are all coated and warmed through, it's ready to serve. Give it one final stir, then garnish with the spring onion and serve immediately.

10 mins

5 mins

DF

Sichuan Lamb

1 tablespoon rapeseed oil

1 green chilli, deseeded and finely chopped

1 medium onion, cut into half-moon slices

large handful of long dried chillies

250g lamb fillet, cut into 0.5 x 2.5cm length slices

pinch of Chinese five-spice powder

1 tablespoon Shaohsing rice wine or dry sherry

2 celery sticks, sliced on the diagonal into 2.5cm pieces

1 tablespoon chilli bean paste

1 tablespoon Chinkiang black rice vinegar or balsamic vinegar

1 tablespoon low-sodium light soy sauce

1 teaspoon chilli oil

handful of roasted peanuts

small handful of fresh coriander stems and leaves, roughly chopped

Calling all spicy food lovers – this moreish dish is perfect made with beef, lamb or even tender goat fillet. For my vegan friends, use smoked tofu slices. The onions provide to counterbalance the spicy hit of the Sichuan peppercorns, and the celery gives a tasty aniseed flavour and delightful crunchy texture. Serve with steamed jasmine rice.

Serves 2 kcal 389 carbs 13.9g protein 31g fat 24.1g

Place a wok over a high heat until smoking and add the rapeseed oil. Add the green chilli, onion and dried chillies and stir-fry for 15 seconds to soften, release their flavours and caramelise at the edges.

Add the lamb fillet and leave for 3 seconds, then toss to cook for 30 seconds. Add the five-spice powder and Shaohsing rice wine or dry sherry. Toss in the celery pieces and stir-fry on a high heat for 30 seconds, then drizzle a dash of water around the edge of the wok to create steam to help it cook.

Season with the chilli bean paste, vinegar, light soy sauce and chilli oil. Add the roasted peanuts and toss all together. Stir in the coriander and serve immediately.

Glossary

Bamboo shoots
These add a crunchy texture to dishes. Boiled bamboo sprouts are also pickled in brine, giving them a sour taste, and in chilli oil, which gives them a spicy taste.

Buckwheat Noodles
Made from 100% buckwheat flour, they contain nutrients such as protein, complex carbohydrates and thiamine and manganese. They are also gluten- and fat-free.

Chilli bean paste
Made from broad beans and chillies that have been fermented with salt to give a deep brown-red sauce. Some versions include fermented soya beans or garlic. Good in soups and braised dishes, it should be used with caution, as some varieties are extremely hot.

Chilli oil
A fiery, orange-red oil made by heating dried red chillies in oil. To make your own, heat groundnut oil in a wok, add dried chilli flakes with seeds and cook for 2 minutes. Take off the heat and leave the chilli to infuse in the oil until completely cooled. Decant into a glass jar and store for a month before using. For a clear oil, pass through a sieve.

Chilli sauce/chilli garlic sauce
A bright red, hot sauce made from chillies, vinegar, sugar and salt. Some varieties are flavoured with garlic and vinegar.

Chinese celery
Chinese celery stalks are slimmer and more tender than the Western variety and the flavour is more intense. Both the stalks and leaves are used.

Chinese leaf/cabbage
This has a delicate, sweet aroma with a mild flavour that disappears when cooked. The white stalk has a crunchy texture and remains succulent even after prolonged cooking. The Koreans mainly use it for kimchi.

Chinese chives (garlic chives)
Long, flat, green leaves with a strong garlic flavour. There are two varieties, one has small yellow flowers at the top, which can be eaten. Both are delicious.

Chinese five-spice powder
A blend of five spices – cinnamon, cloves, Sichuan peppercorns, fennel and star anise – that give the distinctive sour, bitter, pungent, sweet and salty flavours of Chinese cooking. This spice works extremely well with meats and in marinades.

Chinese sausages
These vary in fattiness and sugar content. Though most are made from pork, some use a mixture of offal and belly (and are infused with spices and rice wine). Depending on their dryness they may need to be steam cooked before slicing and adding to stir-fries.

Chinese sesame paste
Made from crushed roasted white sesame seeds blended with toasted sesame oil, it is used with other sauces to flavour dishes. If you cannot find it, you can use tahini instead, but it is a lot lighter in flavour so you will need to add more toasted sesame oil.

Chinese wood ear mushrooms
Dark brown-black fungi with ear-shaped caps. Very crunchy in texture, they do not impart flavour but add colour and crispness. They should be soaked in hot water for 20 minutes before cooking – they will double in size.

Chinkiang black rice vinegar
A strong aromatic vinegar made from fermented rice. The taste is mellow and earthy and it gives dishes a wonderful smoky flavour. Balsamic vinegar makes a good substitute.

Choi sum
A green leafy vegetable with a thick stem and tender leaves that belongs to the Brassica family, it is delicious either steamed or stir-fried. Tenderstem broccoli is a good substitute.

Cinnamon stick/bark
The dried bark of various trees in the Cinnamomum family. It can be used in pieces or ground. Ground adds a sweet woody fragrance.

Congee
Plain soupy rice porridge that can be combined with other ingredients, such as salted peanuts, fermented bean curd, and chilli-pickled bamboo shoots.

Daikon (white radish)
Resembling a large white carrot, this crunchy vegetable has a

peppery taste and pungent smell, and is eaten raw, pickled or cooked. It contains vitamin C and diastase, which aids digestion. Koreans use it to make kimchi.

Deep-fried tofu
Fresh bean curd that has been deep-fried to a golden brown to make it crispy and crunchy on the outside.

Dofu – see Fresh bean curd

Dried Chinese mushrooms
These need to be soaked in hot water for 20 minutes before cooking. They have a strong aroma and a slightly salty taste and therefore complement savoury dishes well.

Dried shrimp
Orange-red and very pungent, these shrimp have been cooked and then dried and salted. To use, soak in hot water for 20 minutes, then drain.

Dried Sichuan chillies/chilli flakes
Hot and fragrant, these chillies are usually sun-dried. You can grind the whole chillies in a pestle and mortar to give flakes.

Dried upward heaven-facing chilli
Also known as 'facing heaven pepper', this medium hot, cone-shaped chilli is used dried as it is too hot to be eaten raw. A good substitute is dried cayenne pepper.

Edamame beans
These are harvested while the beans are still attached to the bushy branches on which they grow (*eda* means 'branches' and *mame* 'beans' in Japanese). High in protein they are cooked whole and the seeds are then squeezed out.

Egg noodles
Made from egg yolk, wheat flour and salt, and available fresh or dried, these come in a variety of thickness and shapes – flat and thin, long and rounded like spaghetti, and flat and coiled in a ball.

Enoki mushrooms
Tiny, white, very thin, long-stemmed mushrooms with a delicate flavour. Used raw, they add texture to salads. Lightly steamed, they are slightly chewy.

Fermented cucumber kimchi
Known as *oi sobagi*, there are two types: wet and dry. Dry has a crunchy texture, the wet a softer one. If you can't find them, use small cucumbers and quickly 'pickle' by adding to fermented kimchi cabbage.

Fermented fish paste
Fish that has been fermented until it has become a salty, smooth paste. A little goes a long way

Fermented salted black beans
Small black soya beans preserved in salt, which must be rinsed in cold water before use. They are used to make black bean sauce.

Fermented yellow bean paste
Made from yellow soybeans, water and salt. A cheat substitute would be hoisin sauce, though this is sweeter and not as salty.

Fish sauce
A light amber liquid extracted from fermented fish and sea salt. The first press – made without additives or sugar – is the most prized.

Fresh bean curd (dofu/tofu)
Described as the 'cheese' of China, this is made from soya bean curd and is quite bland, but takes on the flavour of whatever ingredients it is cooked with. Called tofu in Japan and dofu in Chinese, dofu, it is high in protein and also contains B vitamins, isoflavones and calcium. Available as firm, soft and silken, the firm variety is great in soups, salads and stir-fries. Silken has a cream cheese-like texture. *Dofu gan* is dried firm smoked beancurd.

Gai lan (Chinese broccoli)
Unlike Western green broccoli, *gai lan* comes in several varieties,

some with yellow flowers, though most have large, glossy blue-green leaves with long, thick and crisp chunky stems. A good substitute is Tenderstem broccoli.

Goji berry (Chinese wolfberry)
The deep red, dried fruit of an evergreen shrub. Similar to a raisin, it is sweet and nutritionally rich, and can be eaten raw or cooked.

Hoisin sauce
Made from fermented soya beans, sugar, vinegar, star anise, sesame oil and red rice, this is great used as a marinade and as a dipping sauce.

Jasmine rice
A long-grain white rice originating from Thailand that has a nutty jasmine-scented aroma. You need to rinse it before cooking until the water runs clear to get rid of any excess starch.

Jicama (Mexican yam bean/turnip)
Called *dòush* in China, this is papery yellow on the outside with a creamy white crisp texture inside resembling pear or raw potato. Sweet and starchy in taste, it pairs well with lemon or lime juice. Use crisp Asian pear or pear as a substitute.

Kaffir lime leaves
The leaves of the citrus fruit native to tropical Asia. The leaves emit an intense citrus aroma.

Kimchi
A Korean staple made from salted and fermented Chinese cabbage mixed with Korean radish, Korean dried chilli flakes, spring onions, ginger and *geotgal* (salted seafood).

Korean chilli flakes (gochugaru)
Made by first drying the chillies in the sun, then deseeding and crushing them, these vibrant red flakes impart a spicy taste with a hint of sweetness. A good substitute is dried chilli flakes.

Korean chilli paste (gochujang)
A savoury, sweet, fermented

paste made from Korean red chilli powder, glutinous rice, and salt-and-barley malt powder. Soya beans are also sometimes used.

Korean yellow bean paste
Similar to Chinese yellow bean paste and Japanese miso, this made from fermented soya beans and brine. It is also flavoured with garlic and sesame oil and mixed with Korean chilli paste to produce *samjang*, a sauce that accompanies meat dishes.

Lemongrass (citronella root)
A tough, lemon-scented stalk popular in Thai and Vietnamese cuisines. Look for lemon-green stalks that are tightly formed, firm and heavy with no bruising, tapering to a deeper green towards the end.

Mock duck
A vegetarian ingredient made from wheat gluten, soya, sugar, salt and oil. A good substitute is bean curd or tofu skin.

Mirin
A sweet Japanese rice wine similar to sake, with a lower alcohol content but a higher sugar one (the sugar occurs naturally as a result of the fermentation process).

Miso paste
A thick Japanese paste made from fermented rice, barley, soya beans, salt and a fungus called *kojikin*. Sweet, earthy, fruity and salty, it comes in many varieties depending on the types of grains used.

Mung bean noodles
Made from the starch of green mung beans and water, these noodles come in various thicknesses, vermicelli being the thinnest. To use, soak in hot water for 5–6 minutes before cooking. If using in soups or deep-frying, no pre-soaking is necessary. They become translucent when cooked.

Mushroom oyster sauce – see oyster sauce

Nori (dried seaweed)
Sold in thin sheets, this is usually roasted over a flame until it turns black or purple-green. Used as a garnish or to wrap sushi, once opened, a pack must be sealed and stored in an airtight container or it loses its crispness. If this happens, just roast the sheets over an open flame for a few seconds until crisp.

Oyster mushrooms
Soft and chewy with a slight oyster taste, this white, yellow or grey oyster shaped fungi is moist and fragrant.

Oyster sauce
A seasoning sauce made from oyster extract that can also be used as a marinade. A vegetarian variety is also available. It is very salty, so taste the dish before adding.

Pad Thai noodles
Flat noodles, 5mm wide, made from rice. They need to be soaked in hot water for 5 minutes before cooking.

Pak choy
A vegetable with broad green leaves, which taper to white stalks. Crisp and crunchy, it can be boiled, steamed or stir-fried.

Panko breadcrumbs
Made from bread without crusts, these Japanese breadcrumbs have a crisp texture.

Persian cucumbers
Small, thin-skinned cucumbers, 10–15cm long, with soft, tiny seeds, Mild and sweet.

Potato flour
A smooth, gluten-free flour made from potatoes that are steamed, dried and then ground. It gives wonderful crispness when used to coat ingredients before frying.

Ramen
Noodles, invented in China, that are used in Japanese noodle soups. They come in various thicknesses and shapes, but most are made from wheat flour, salt, water and *kansui* (alkaline mineral water), the latter ingredient gives the noodles a yellow hue and a firmer texture.

Red miso paste – see Miso paste

Rice vinegar
A clear (white), mild vinegar made from fermented rice. Cider vinegar can be used as a substitute. Chinese black rice vinegar is a rich, aromatic vinegar that is used in braised dishes and sauces, and with noodles. When cooked, it gives a smoky flavour with a mellow and earthy taste. Balsamic vinegar makes a good substitute.

Sake
A fermented Japanese drink made from polished rice that is brewed in a similar way to wine. Its alcohol content ranges from 15–20%.

Sambal oelek
A staple in Malaysian and Thai cooking that is used to add heat to dishes. It is made from fiery red chillies, vinegar and salt. A little goes a long way.

Sesame seeds
These oil-rich seeds add a nutty taste and a delicate texture to many Asian dishes. Available in black, white/yellow and red varieties, toasted and untoasted.

Shaohsing rice wine
Made from rice, millet and yeast that has been aged for 3–5 years, it takes the 'odour' or 'rawness' out of meats and fish and gives a bittersweet finish. Dry sherry makes a good substitute.

Shiitake mushrooms
These large, nutrient-rich, dark brown umbrella-shaped fungi are prized for their culinary and medicinal properties. The dried variety needs to be soaked in water for 20 minutes before cooking.

Shimeji (beech) mushrooms
These come in white or brown

varieties, and are characterised by long stems and tight concave caps.

Shichimi pepper flakes/Japanese chilli flakes (nana-iro togarashi)
A Japanese spice that contains ground red chilli pepper, ground Sichuan peppercorns, roasted orange peel, white and black sesame seeds, hemp seeds, nori and ground ginger.

Shishito peppers
Small, finger-long, thin-skinned sweet Asian peppers that turn from green to red, although they are usually harvested while still green. The tip is also known as *shizi* (lion in Mandarin), hence its name. Before cooking, you need to poke with a hole to prevent hot air building up inside and bursting the chilli.

Shrimp paste
A dry, smooth paste made by adding salt to shrimp or fish broth, this is then stored overnight, drained and sun dried. The mixture is then ground and left to ferment in an earthenware jar. A good paste should be dark deep purple.

Sichuan peppercorns
Known as 'Hua jiao' in Mandarin or 'flower pepper', these have a pungent, citrusy aroma. They can be wok-roasted, cooked in oil to flavour the oil, or mixed with salt as a condiment.

Somen noodles
Very fine, dried wheat flour noodles, also known as 'longevity' noodles, and traditionally eaten on festivals and birthdays.

Soy sauce
Made from wheat and fermented soya beans, soy sauce is available in dark and light varieties. Dark soy sauce is aged a lot longer than the light variety, and is mellower and less salty. Light soy sauce is used in China instead of salt. Wheat-free varieties, called tamari, are available, though it is quite salty.

You can also buy low-sodium varieties.

Soybean noodles
Thin, gluten-free dried noodles that are rich in protein, and low in fat. They yield about double the amount of wheat flour noodles once rehydrated.

Sriracha chilli sauce
A hot sauce made from chilli peppers, distilled vinegar, garlic, salt and sugar. It is named after the coastal town of Si Racha, Eastern Thailand.

Star anise
The fruit of a small evergreen plant, these are called *bajio* or 'eight horns' in Chinese. They have a distinct aniseed flavour and are one of the ingredients found in Chinese five-spice powder.

Taiwanese nine-pagoda leaf basil
This herb has a clove, lemon and liquorice scent. Use Thai sweet basil as a substitute.

Tamari – see Soy sauce

Thai aubergines
Thai varieties are smaller than Western aubergines (often no bigger than a golf ball), and are usually green and white. The smallest are known as pea aubergines, the long thin purple varieties as Asian aubergines.

Tian mian jiang (sweet bean sauce)
A thick, smooth, opaque dark brown sauce made from wheat flour, salt, sugar and fermented yellow soybeans. Hoisin is sometimes used as an alternative though it is much sweeter.

Toasted sesame oil
Made from white pressed and toasted sesame seeds, this oil is used as a flavouring/seasoning and is not suitable for use as a cooking oil since it burns easily. The flavour is intense, so use sparingly.

Tofu – see Fresh bean curd

Vermicelli mung bean noodles – see Mung bean noodles

Vermicelli rice noodle
Similar to vermicelli mung bean noodles, they come in many different widths and varieties. Before cooking, soak in hot water for 5 minutes. If using in salads, soak for 20 minutes. If using in a soup, add them dry.

Water chestnuts
The roots of an aquatic plant that grows in freshwater ponds, marshes and lakes, and in slow-moving rivers and streams. Unpeeled, they resemble a chestnut in shape and colouring. They have a firm, crunchy texture.

Wheat flour noodles
Thin, white dried noodles. Do not confuse these with thick Japanese udon noodles.

Yellow bean sauce
Made from fermented yellow soya beans, dark brown sugar and rice wine, this is a very popular flavouring ingredient in Sichuan and Hunan province in China. It also makes a great marinade for meats. Yellow bean paste is a thicker consistency and is used in marinades and as a flavouring in many savoury dishes.

Zha cai (Sichuan vegetable)
A popular Sichuan pickled mustard vegetable used in hot and sour soups and dan dan noodles. The knobbly fist-sized stems are salted, pressed, dried and then covered in hot chilli paste and fermented in an earthenware jar (similar to that of Korean kimchi). The taste is spicy, salty and sour with a crunchy texture. Excess salt can be removed by soaking in fresh water. Usually sold in vacuum packs either whole or ready sliced.

Index

Acknowledgments

I owe a big thank you to Kyle Cathie and my editor, Judith Hannam. Writing a book can be a scary process, sometimes full of self-doubt, but I am truly blessed to have your belief and support of my work.

This book could not have happened without my literary agent, Heather Holden Brown, who helped make it a reality. Thank you, also, to Toby Eady and Xinran Xue for being my cheerleaders and always guiding me.

A huge thanks to all my fans for continuing to support me on my culinary journey, this book is for you. I have tried to incorporate as many vegan and vegetarian recipes as possible, as this is something I am often asked, and half the book is veggie friendly. I hope you enjoy the recipes as much as I have enjoyed creating them for you. I am indebted and ever grateful for your love.

I am extremely honoured to have the friendship of chef Tom Kerridge. I adore, admire and respect your work greatly. It means so much to me to have your support.

The talented team at Kyle Books are just incredible – xie xie to Editorial Assistant Hannah Coughlin and my copy editor Barbara Dixon (who I have had the pleasure of working with for many years now), for your amazing attention to detail. Thank you to Caroline Clark for the funky design of the book. I raise more than a glass to the incredible Tamin Jones for the photography, to the talented Aya Nishimura for the beautiful food styling, and of course the one and only Wei Tang for the props, as well as special thanks to Nic Jones and Gemma John for the production of the book.

My agent and friend, Kate Heather, you have championed me and continue to support me through thick and thin, helping me so much whilst juggling babies and family life. Thank you for all your hard work and belief from your no.1 daughter.

Thank you to Michael Kagan at ICM Talent and assistant Colin Burke in US for continuing to support my career and for believing in me.

Thanks to all the powers at BBC, ITV, Food Network UK and US, the Cooking Channel and NBC for continuing to give me opportunities and allowing me to share my cooking on TV.

To all my family near or far, especially my mum and dad, it has not always been a 'lovely' life for us. I wouldn't be here without you and I am so proud of how far we have come as a family. This book is also for my three grandmas – Wu, Huang and Carmel Longhurst – you are my angels, looking out for me, giving me love, strength and inspiration.

To Jamie, my husband, I drive you crazy with my Stir Crazy. Thank you for putting up with everything I dish out – you are my everything.